A GATHERING OF WORDS

A TRAIN OF THOUGHT

Forty Years Workin' on the Railroad

Garret –

*Best wishes – Hope
you enjoy the book!*

Terry Beck

3-6-14

TERRY BECK

A Gathering of Words – A Train of Thought

Copyright © 2013 by Terry Beck

Mary Beth Smith
Park Cities Publishing
3032 Mockingbird Lane
Dallas, TX 75205

Ordering Information:
Quantity sales. Special discounts are available on quantity purchases by corporations, associations, and others. For details, contact the publisher at the address above.

Printed in the United States of America

To my loving wife, Amber

I told you I was writing a book!

TABLE OF CONTENTS

FOREWORD

———————

Sip the stories in this book like you would a cool beer down by the creek, or if you're like me, in your favorite easy chair. Leave those "reading" glasses where they are, and put on your "listening" glasses, because Terry Beck is a consummate teller of stories. Here, much to our good fortune, he has troubled to write them down for you in the purely conversational manner of just passing an afternoon on the porch with your best friend.

I'm not a railroad man (though my dad was a car knocker for the Santa Fe), but old hands will recognize the machinery and, I'm pretty sure, the flavor of some of the shenanigans that unfold here, while the uninitiated will learn some of the colorful backdrop of railroading as it was in the '70's and '80's. Terry has a knack for humanizing what might otherwise seem like mighty tiring work. Whether he's falling from the roadbed into a rushing river, or trying to find a home for a dog found chained to the tracks, ol' Terry is keenly cognizant that every railroading lesson learned is a life lesson as well.

This book frames Terry's amusing, compelling railroading experiences with updates on the toll that long, irregular hours inevitably took on life at home with the wife and kids. His family stands as living proof that behind every successful man stands a loving, understanding wife. In his often self-deprecating, always charming manner, Terry Beck makes the case that when all is said and done, being a good railroad man is pretty much the same as being a good man. He is one of those, and that's a crosstie you can stake your rails to.

Jerry Stubblefield
Asheville, NC
December 2013

PREFACE

I was born in the smallish Texas town of Brownwood. Unless your folks owned a business or a farm/ranch there were few really "good paying" jobs in town. One of those "good" jobs was with the Atchison Topeka and Santa Fe Railroad. When I was a child, our neighbor worked for the railroad and I loved listening to his stories as he spoke of his railroading adventures. I remember telling Mom that when I grew up I wanted to be a railroader. She smiled down at me, patted me on the head and said, "Well sweetheart, you'll have to make up your mind, 'cause you can't do both!"

I did get a job on the grand old Santa Fe Railroad on June 25, 1971. I hired out as a gandy dancer driving spikes. Over the next forty years with the railroad I worked as a machine operator, a gang foreman, a track supervisor, brakeman, conductor, locomotive engineer, safety supervisor, manager of safety and rules, trainmaster and assistant superintendant. During this time I was fortunate to meet and work with some of the most interesting men and women in the country. They were not all intellects, and they were not all hard workers, but they were all interesting and sometimes a little different.

In my early years on the railroad, the "old heads", who had already put in over forty years, shared stories of their careers with me. I was amazed, even if half the stories were true, by the truly unique and exciting lives these folks had lived. Then during my own long career on the railroad, I became part of railroad history and, for better or for worse, became a character in, as well as a teller of, railroad stories. Railroaders love to talk, and for years, even after retiring, I would share my stories with anybody that would listen.

Back in 2009, I looked around and noticed that all those old railroad story tellers who came before me were gone, and a lot of my own generation was also gone. I began to realize that a time would come when

I, and those like me, would no longer be here to breathe life into these stories. In particular, I wanted my children and grandchildren to know what had been on my tired old mind. That's when I began writing a journal containing as many stories about the railroad as I could recall. I also began putting my personal thoughts and philosophies down on paper. Later I shared some of my stories through several modes of social media, and to my surprise, there were folks that claimed they enjoyed the stories - Even those who had never had an active interest in railroads or railroading.

Finally, as more friends and family urged me on, I reluctantly began putting together a series of books. *A Gathering Of Words - A Train Of Thought*, a collection of railroad stories, is the first in my series. I am not a railroad expert. I am a railroader that knows a little about a lot of things on the railroad. You won't find a lot of statistical, detailed information in this book. You will find reflections about the railroading souls of yesterday that I had the pleasure of sharing history with. The stories are mostly happy, funny stories, but like life, railroading wasn't always smiles and laughter, and some stories reflect that.

I want to thank my faithful family and friends who have supported and pushed me to complete something I thought well beyond my capabilities. In particular, I want to thank my old friend and classmate, talented playwright/author and wordmaster Jerry Stubblefield, for his tutelage and patient support. I also want to thank another classmate, friend and publisher Mary Beth Smith, of Park Cities Publishing for her tireless work and assistance in making this book a possibility. Thank you to all!

Friends and Family Always!

Terry Beck
Burleson, TX
December 2013

A GATHERING OF WORDS

A TRAIN OF THOUGHT
Forty Years Workin' on the Railroad

Day to Day, Year to Year, Boy to Man

PART I

———————◆———————

He awakened in the morning to the sound of the rustling leaves of the cottonwood tree outside the open window of his bedroom. The distant laughter and the familiar sounds of his neighborhood friends playing could be heard over the dull roar of the evaporative air cooler in the window across the room. He threw back the cover and rushed into the kitchen to get a quick bowl of cereal because he was running late. He hoped that he hadn't missed anything, although every day was always pretty much the same as any other day.

Having quickly finished the cereal, he slipped on a pair of shorts, all that he would need on this mid-summer day, and rushed out to join his friends and brothers. He knew what his boundaries were, even though there were no fences. He knew every-one's name for blocks around and they knew his. After all, they were neighbors. He had no natural fear of anything or anyone in the neighborhood except wasp nests, goat head stickers and red ant beds. After several hours of rompin' and stompin', the unmistakable sound of his dad's old Chevrolet pickup could be heard coming down the street, which meant lunch time with the family. The race was on to see who could get home, wash their hands and be seated at the kitchen table first.

After lunch, he was back outside riding bicycles for miles, although there was just as much enjoyment to be found in giant cardboard boxes, trees, big piles of dirt or sand, and deep holes in the ground. As the day sped to an end, the shadows became longer and the mouth-watering scent of suppertime meals began to drift across the neigh-borhood. Soon the shrill whistle of his mom could be heard and he headed home, smelling of sweat, peppered with dirt, and grease still on his hands from fixing the chain on his bicycle.

Supper was enjoyed as a family, then he was off to take a bath, unless it was his time to wash dishes. After the rotation of baths was completed in the one bathroom home, everyone gathered in their spot in the living room and watched their favorite television show on their brand new black and white television. It was during this time that any-one who complained of having a sticker in their foot could have it removed, usually with a needle and/or tweezers. Personally, he preferred his mother's technique over his dad's if it came down to using the needle to remove the sticker from the tough soles of his feet.

Then it was bedtime, a little too early he thought, but after making a frail argument to watch one more show, he went to bed. He would lie in bed next to the open window and listen to the rustling leaves of the cottonwood tree until he drifted to sleep.

And then came school. There were a few adjustments that came with school. He had to wear shoes and a shirt to school, and then keep them on all day. He had to have permission to talk in class, no matter how important or neat he thought the subject matter was. But he did learn, he gained a multitude of new friends, the food was al-most as good as at home (the homemade rolls may have been better), and he learned a new word, 'girlfriend'.

Junior High School was a learning experience that was not limited to the classroom. Girls seemed to be more of a distraction. Sports began to increase in popularity, not only to the athletes but to observers as well. The girls just kept getting prettier, and they could no longer outrun the boys, or at least they no longer wanted to try. He had more friends than ever before, but he noticed that some of them were finding new interests and moving in different directions. Or, possibly he was the one moving in a different direction. He was gaining a new independence, and in doing so began making decisions without the direct guidance of his parents. Most decisions they would have been proud of, although some it was best they never knew about. Then, in his last year of Junior High, he achieved an unbelievable goal: a 1956 Nash Ambassador. Goodbye, school bus.

Then came High School, probably one of the highlights of his life. With higher levels of education came even more distractions, and the girls still kept getting prettier. He did well in the classes he liked, but in the classes he didn't like, he dragged his feet and became lazy. His grades were average, but looking back, he knows they could have been much better. Something new came into the picture about this time – Love. He fell in love several times during this period. At the time it seemed like it was true love, *and it probably was, but he would find out much later in life what true love really was.*

There was so much for him to remember about this period of his life: the sports victories, the music, the dances, the dates, the teachers, the coaches, the classmates and the beginning of manhood. Probably the greatest reward of these years was the friends and the bonds that he thought would last forever.

With college came true independence, as he left home for the first time. He had traded home life for dorm life. Dorm life was not nearly as crowded. The independence of college brought out the best in the majority of students, but not him. The academic laziness that had begun in high school would worsen in college. He did just enough to get by and stay off of scholastic probation. He no longer participated in sports. He had found that the friendships that he thought would last forever were fading. He had started dabbling in several different modes of intoxication. After a year away from home, he moved back and enrolled in the hometown college and began working part time. He had forgotten what it felt like to be a winner. He had forgotten about the binding camaraderie of high school. He had forgotten about the thrill of a girl saying "yes" as a date to the big dance. He had temporarily lost the close connection of family. His rookie season as an adult was not his best.

FIRST DAYS. TOUGH DAYS. LEARNING DAYS.

On June 25, 1971 I went to work for the Santa Fe Railroad in Brownwood, Texas to make a little money before going back to school in September. I hired on as a gandy dancer, or snipe, which was a laborer position whose proper name was trackman. The first gang on which I worked was called a rail joint gang, working from Brownwood to Sweetwater. Back then the rail portion of the railroad was made up of pieces of rail, with each piece being thirty-three feet long. Each rail was bolted together to the next with two heavy bars and six large bolts and this was called a joint. Our task was to spray each joint with oil, inspect the joint bars for breaks or cracks, and make certain each bolt was tightened.

The gang was made up of an oil spray machine pushed on a cart by one man, with two more men out in front walking and spraying oil on each joint. Behind the spray operation were two bolt machines that would either tighten the bolts, or remove them if the bar was broken and replace it with a new bar and bolts. Naturally, being the youngest of the gang, I was one of the oil prayers and got to work on the downwind side so I was pretty well lubricated by the end of each day.

Things were going pretty well my first day, right up to the point where my foreman hollered out that it was break time. Just as I sat down to rest, the foreman told me that we were going to need one more joint bar and wanted me to walk back to the road crossing about three quarters of a mile back, and bring a bar from the supply stack. I walked back to the crossing and picked up one of the 50 Lb. bars, threw it up on my shoulder and walked back to the gang. As I dropped it to the ground the Foreman hollered "Damn, Beck! We needed an outside bar and you brought an inside bar. Take this bar back and get the proper bar."

So, I threw the bar back up on my shoulder and walked back to the crossing. As I dropped the bar to the ground, shoulders aching, I looked toward the stack of bars -- they were all the same. The light bulb came on: There was no such thing as an inside or outside bar. I picked up the bar once again and carried it back to the gang and without saying a word, threw the bar to the ground at which point the foreman yelled, "Break's over! Back to work."

In an hour or so we stopped for lunch. We found a large shade tree just off the right-of-way with plush green rye grass and settled in for some lunch and much needed rest. It was just going to be rest for me because I hadn't brought a lunch. I suppose I had thought we would eat at a Dairy Queen or something. Oh well, I would know better the next day.

Thirty minutes later the foreman hollered that it was time to go back to work and everybody gathered up their stuff and walked back toward the track. I got up, stretched and started to walk out of the shade when the foreman walked over to me and handed me a sandwich and a cup of water and said, "Here, take my extra sandwich and this water. And take another fifteen minutes." He paused and said, "You're going to be all right, Beck."

And so it went as we walked from Brownwood to Sweetwater over the next month.

WEED MOWING DUDE

B y August of 1971, I had just finished walking from Brownwood to
Sweetwater with the rail joint gang in a little over a month. It was
Saturday and I was home wondering if I should buy a new, sturdier pair
of boots when the phone rang. It was the Santa Fe Division Engineer's
office wanting to know if I would be interested in a machine operator
position. I was planning on returning to school at Howard Payne College in September, but asked how much that job would pay. They said
the job would pay a couple of hundred dollars more a month than I was
making on my present position, so I decided to take the position. I was
told to report Monday morning to Roadmaster Scott in Sweetwater as a
machine operator on a weed mower (tractor).

I reported to Roadmaster Scott Monday morning and was told that
my machine was loaded in a boxcar that had been moved to a loading
dock. He instructed me to unload the tractor and begin mowing the
right-of-way in and around Sweetwater. Contrary to popular belief,
not every male born in the state of Texas knows how to operate a tractor, and I was living proof. I had never been on a tractor in my life, but
didn't think the roadmaster wanted to hear that.

I found the boxcar with my tractor loaded inside. As I opened one of
the side doors and viewed the tractor with attached mower inside the
boxcar, I wondered how in the heck they get that thing loaded and
even more important, how I was going to get it unloaded. If you've
seen those whiskey bottles with a schooner built inside, and wondered
how anyone could have done such a thing, you know the feeling I had
at that moment.

After hours of working and head scratching and finally figuring out that I was going to have to open the side door on the other side of the boxcar, in order to maneuver the tractor to where the mower was sticking out the opposite side of the car, I triumphantly drove the tractor out of the boxcar. Needless to say, by then I knew what every lever, button and pedal did on the machine; I was indeed a weed mower operator.

I spent several days mowing in and around Sweetwater with only a few happenings of interest. On the second day, I noticed some belts and bolts that had worked loose on my tractor. I had yet to build up a good arsenal of tools, but I saw a signal maintainer's truck nearby. I walked over and was about to open one of the toolbox doors on the utility bed of the truck, when someone hollered for me to stop. It was the signal maintainer, who asked what I was doing. I told him I just wanted to borrow a wrench. He told me I should never open any of the tool boxes on his truck. He slowly opened one of the tool box doors. Inside was a live rattle snake, about four feet long. He explained that as he found these snakes, he would catch them and keep them in his tool boxes. He went on to say that everyone who worked in that area knew of his habits and that he didn't have a problem with people stealing his tools.

After finishing up mowing at Sweetwater, The roadmaster told me to move my tractor to Ballinger and start mowing on the San Angelo District. When I asked how I was going to get the mower to Ballinger, his response was "Drive it. It's just sixty miles or so!" So, bright and early the next morning I began my trip to Ballinger. About two hours into the trip, bouncing down the shoulder of the highway at a blazing ten or fifteen miles an hour, I came across a roadside park. At this park was a white van with "San Angelo State University Cheerleaders" printed on the side. There were seven or eight cheerleading-type gals sitting around tables, eating and talking.

My weed mower was almost identical to those used by the Highway Department, so I wheeled in and mowed every inch of the park. I even picked up some trash and placed it in the trash cans near the tables. It was probably the best that park had looked in years.

The rest of the trip was uneventful other than occasionally, due to sheer boredom, I would drop the mower down and mow a strip a mile or two long down the edge of the highway.

I'm sure the Texas Highway Department appreciated my help.

FOREMAN DAY - FOREMAN KNIGHT

Late that year, I received a call from the Santa Fe Railroad and was instructed to report to an engineering gang working in Dallas, Texas. I had been an employee of the railroad for only a few months, and had been promoted to the position of machine operator, although I didn't have enough seniority to hold that position at the time. I was therefore assigned as a trackman to this particular gang. This gang was made up of a foreman, a machine operator and four trackmen. The gang was called a surfacing gang. Its sole purpose was to raise, tamp and realign track in order to provide trains with a smoother, faster riding surface.

This gang, headquartered at Santa Fe's East Dallas Freight Yard near Fair Park, was working on an old branch line called the Hale Cement Line. There were several large industries serviced by this line, most of which were cement plants, as the name would suggest. Despite being only a few miles from downtown Dallas, this old branch line was pretty much in the wilderness.

On the morning I was to report to duty, I spent several hours just trying to find the freight yard. After locating the yard, it took me another hour to find the on-duty point of my gang. Being from Brownwood, Texas, I had never really considered myself a "country boy", but after three stress filled hours of trying to figure out where the heck I was going in Dallas, I felt pretty "country."

I was elated to see the gang in the distance - four yellow hats and one white hat. Everyone wore yellow hard hats except the foreman who wore white. I approached the white hat prepared to take whatever I had coming for being three hours late. He was an older fellow with silver hair, and large, dark- framed glasses. He was smoking a pipe, which gave him an air of sophistication. As I approached, a big smile came to his face and he extended his hand. As we shook hands, he told me he was glad I had found them so easily. He proceeded to introduce me to each of my fellow gang members. As he introduced each man, he would give his complete name, where he was from and a tidbit of his personal history.

We spent a little more time gathering some material for the job site, then stopped for lunch. We sat under a bridge near a small creek and opened our lunch boxes. The old foreman was very personable. He asked where I was from, about my family, my education and what, if any, ambitions I might have. He then told me a little about my coworkers and then some about himself. He had worked for the Santa Fe Railroad over forty years and was going to retire in a few months. He spoke of how he would miss the railroad, but that mostly he would miss the many friends with whom he had shared his railroad career. He spoke slowly and deliberately. His conversations were articulate and sincere.

The work was hard, and different from anything I had ever done before. The foreman seemed to take me under his wing for a few hours each day for the rest of that first week. Not only would he tell me what to do, he would also explain the reasons for doing certain things. He wouldn't let anyone stay on one task for an extended time. He would rotate us from one activity to another. He explained to me that his intent was to prevent boredom due to performing the same task all day, to teach each man every aspect of the job, and to eventually make his job as foreman easier.

Each day at quitting time we would return to the rail yard. The foreman had a large camper trailer parked on the railroad property. On the first day he had made a point to introduce me to his wife, who was staying with him that week. She was also very personable and would send homemade cookies with the foreman each morning, with instructions to see that we all received all we wanted.

The second week began much as the first week except there were no homemade cookies. I later found out that his wife would come down with him from Oklahoma every other week. We began that day where we had stopped the Friday before. Things seemed a little different for some reason. Shortly after we began work, the old foreman picked up his lunch bucket and without saying a word, began to walk down the track in front of us until he finally disappeared from view. My fellow workers never missed a lick. Work went on as if the boss was standing there with us. I was really impressed with how much everybody knew about the work, and the pride they seemed to take in what they were doing. After an hour or so, with the foreman still gone, I finally asked where he went. I was told that he was walking ahead to see what work was ahead of us.

About an hour before quitting time we came to a large clump of Johnson grass that had been pulled up and placed on the rail. We worked to that point, loaded all the tools on the machine and the machine operator sounded the air horn on the machine. In a few minutes, the foreman came walking back toward us. As he walked between the rails he seemed to be zigzagging a little. Nobody said a word. He climbed onto the machine with the rest of us and we headed back to the truck. When we arrived back at the truck, the old foreman walked over and got in on the passenger side rather than the driver's seat as he had the week before. There wasn't much said as the machine operator drove us back to the yard.

That's the way it went all week. The foreman would walk off down the track, we would work our way down the track until we came to a clump of Johnson grass on the rail. The foreman had even taught everyone on the gang how to do all his paperwork, timekeeping forms and daily work reports. He would sign any forms requiring a signature before work each morning, and we would fill them out and send them off at the yard office each afternoon.

The next week the foreman's wife was back, and so was our foreman. It was just like the first week. He amazed me with his knowledge. At lunch we would all sit and listen to his many railroad stories. Every day he would ask how my folks back in Brownwood were doing, or how some of the other guys' family members were doing. He would talk about all of the good things that the railroad could provide if we would just stick with it.

That's the way it continued. The weeks his wife was there, he never took a drink. The weeks she wasn't there, even though we never saw him take a drink, he was a different man. I have never learned as much as

I did in the two months that I worked with that foreman. He shared more than just knowledge with me. He shared his philosophies and seemed to sincerely want to help me better myself.

Although he never said anything himself, I later found out that he had been a roadmaster and was destined to move on up into higher management positions. I asked if his drinking was the reason for getting out of management. I was told that he didn't have a drinking problem back then; Instead, he had come back to spend more time with his wife and son.

I asked when his drinking started. They told me that he started drinking shortly after his twenty-one year old son died....his son Terry.

PACK A BAG

In March of 1972, my ninth month of employment with the Santa Fe Railroad, I was working as a machine operator in Dallas, Texas. I received a call from the division engineer's office and was asked if I would be interested in entering the Student Foreman Program. I explained that I really had plans to go back to school at Howard Payne College the next semester, but was curious as to what the pay would be on that position. I was told that it would pay several hundred more dollars a month than my present position. Already making what I felt was good money, I thought about it for maybe ten seconds and then told them I would take the position.

My first assignment as Student foreman was with Roadmaster Scott in Brownwood, Texas. Having worked on his territory before as both a trackman and a weed mower operator, I felt comfortable with the assignment. Mr. Scott was a firm but fair supervisor from whom I could learn a great deal. It would be nice to be back in my hometown both emotionally and financially.

He assigned me to the Brownwood section gang. This was a ten man gang, half of which worked in the Brownwood switching yard, with the other half working out on the main line track between Brownwood and Lawn, Texas and between Brownwood and Comanche, Texas. I was told to work with the yard gang.

The yard gang was working in the roundhouse area where locomotives were fueled and serviced. This was long before environmental regulations required drip pans and facilities to prevent the diesel and oil from leaking onto the ground. Our assignment was to shovel all the oil soaked gravel and soil from around the roundhouse tracks and replace it with clean gravel. For three days I was on a shovel in this mess. Starting on the fourth morning, Mr. Scott drove up to our work location and asked how things were going. I told him I realized I was there to learn and to become a better railroader, but that I had pretty much figured out how to use the shovel and was ready to move on to other things.

Mr. Scott smiled, or at least it looked kind of like a smile, and told me to grab my bag and come with him. I wasn't sure what he meant by "bag" but I told him I didn't have a bag. He just looked at me and with a nod of his head and a grin, told me to get in his truck. As we were driving through the freight yard he told me he was going to catch a train and ride it to Sweetwater. He wanted me to drive there and pick him up, and that if all went well we would return to Brownwood that evening.

He informed me the train would not arrive for another hour or so, which would allow him time to drive up to the White Mines Rock Crusher to check on another gang he had working on that industry's tracks. As we arrived at the rock crusher, Mr. Scott parked behind a building, out of sight of the gang. We got out of the truck and walked to the corner of the building and peeked around the corner at the work site. There stood the gang all gathered around the foreman. Charlie, the foreman, would talk a little while and then the gang would just burst out laughing; then Charlie would talk a little more and again they would all begin to laugh. We observed the laugh fest for about five minutes, and I felt uncomfortable knowing that poor old Charlie was about to feel the wrath of Roadmaster Scott.

We walked from behind the building right up behind Charlie, who still had his back turned to us, and Mr. Scott tapped him on the shoulder and said, "What the hell are you doing Charlie?"

Without a second's pause Charlie answered, "Having a safety meeting, Mr. Scott. Does anybody else have any questions?"

Mr. Scott just shook his head and told Charlie to get back to work. We walked through the work site, inspecting the work that had been ac-complished to that point. As we got back in the truck and were driving back to the depot to catch the train, I asked why he had been so lenient on Charlie when he knew that they were not having a safety meeting.

Mr. Scott said that anybody that could lie that fast deserved a break. He continued by saying that he had just scared the crap out of old Charlie. Any further punishment would be wasted because Charlie knew that he had screwed up and been caught. He said the situation had been corrected and that any further punishment would probably do more harm than good.

Mr. Scott boarded the train and told me to head for Sweetwater. I arrived in Sweetwater and drove to the depot and found out from the train dispatcher that the train would not be arriving for a little while longer. I decided, rather than just sitting there at the depot, I would drive outside town a few miles, find the tracks and wait for the train to pass. I found the track and pulled under a shade tree and waited for the train. Thirty minutes passed, then another thirty minutes passed and finally I saw the headlight of a train coming. I got out of the truck and walked over near the track to watch the train pass and let Mr. Scott see how efficient I was.

I watched as the headlight got larger and larger. Finally the train blew by me and my heart skipped a beat; It was a Union Pacific train. I had been waiting for over an hour on the wrong tracks. I hopped back in the truck and drove as fast as I could back to the depot. There in front of the depot sitting on the curb was Roadmaster Scott. He rose slowly, stowed his bag in the back of the truck, got in the truck on the passenger side, turned his head toward me and just stared. After what seemed like an eternity, he turned his head facing the windshield, sighed and said "Let's head back to Brownwood."

It was awfully quiet as I battled with the thought of whether to say anything about why I was late. Just as I was about to apologize for my being late, the dispatcher came on the radio calling Mr. Scott. He advised that there had just been a major derailment in the Sweetwater Yard. We returned to the yard only to be greeted by a really ugly derailment involving fifteen or twenty rail cars and damaging or destroying four yard tracks.

We, and about fifty others, worked on that derailment through the rest of the day, through that night and through the next day. At 6:00 p.m., Mr. Scott suggested that we get rooms and get some rest before heading back to Brownwood. In the room, without a change of clothes, toothbrush or any toiletries, I took off my clothes, stood them over in the corner of the room and took a thirty minute shower. The next morning, after receiving a 4:00 a.m. wake-up call from Mr. Scott, I put on the clothes that were still standing in the corner of the room. There is nothing more uncomfortable than to be clean and rested and put on clothes that had over forty-eight hours of dry sweat and dirt clinging to every thread.

As we walked to the truck Mr. Scott turned to me with a look of pity, or possibly disgust, and said, "You know, you could probably get a pretty good bag at Montgomery Ward, if you think it would be worth the effort."

I bought a bag that very day and for the better part of forty years it was always packed, stocked and available.

OKLAHOMA JACK

I was now twenty-three years old. It was only my second year with the railroad, so I had a lot of learning to do. Since the Santa Fe Railroad had seen fit to promote me to a student foreman's position in hopes of training me for a first line supervisor's job, I was sent from job to job over Texas and Oklahoma, with each job being different, and never staying in one location long enough to become comfortable. It amazed me that there were so many unique personalities across the railroad, with so much to offer on one hand, and so much to forget on the other.

One such personality was an old-head track supervisor in Oklahoma by the name of Jack. There was also a track supervisor in North Texas whose name was Jack, so this fellow was known as Oklahoma Jack. I had been assigned to work with him because he had suffered an injury to his back, or possibly his knees. It has been a few years ago, but I do recall he was hampered by an injury of some type.

Oklahoma Jack patrolled the Oklahoma track between Ardmore and Purcell, inspecting track and managing the workforce within that area. At that time, the track supervisors patrolled the track in motorcars. These motorcars would only run on the track and had room for two riders and a few hand tools. It had a windshield in front, but was open on both sides and the back, and had a metal roof. While one man could set the motor car off and on the track, because Jack was injured, they assigned me to him in order to set the motor car on and off as needed, and to learn about his job, his responsibilities and the art of track inspection.

Oklahoma Jack was a fascinating man. I was amazed by his intellect concerning not only the railroad, but all things in general. I recognized very quickly that this was a man I could learn from, and possibly use as a model for some of my own railroad techniques. He was very quick to point out that his formal education had ended in the eighth grade, but that he had supplemented his education by reading everything he could get his hands on, every day of every week of every year. He would very quickly deny that he was intelligent, but would always say, "I'm really not all that smart, but I am very well informed." I quickly became very close to Jack and trusted his every word and action.

One cool crisp morning, Jack and I were patrolling track in the motorcar, traveling northbound coming into Pauls Valley, Oklahoma. As we came around a long curve we could see for several miles ahead of us because of the straight track heading up a hill before Pauls Valley. I looked ahead, and could see a train headlight coming over the hill moving southbound. I quickly looked over at Jack, tapped his arm and pointed ahead to the engine headlight. He looked ahead and nodded an acknowledgement. I felt us pick up speed as he moved the throttle to the full speed position. Going uphill with two men aboard, the motorcar would only move at about 35-MPH. Trains operated in that location at 55-MPH.

As we chugged up the hill, the headlight of the train got larger by the second. I would look at the train, then look at Jack, then look at the train and back to Jack. Even as the train got closer, Jack was calm and didn't seem to be overly concerned. I, on the other hand was getting a little nervous. I didn't know much, but I did know that there were only two places that a motorcar could be set off the track properly. One was at a road crossing and the other was a motorcar setoff pad built at strategic locations for setting motorcars off the track. I also knew that there were no road crossings immediately ahead of us, but that there was a motorcar set off at the depot in Pauls Valley.

The train came closer, and still Jack kept his hand on the throttle and appeared completely calm. I began to think Jack knew something I didn't. Either the train was going to stop for some reason, or it was going to take the switch to a branch line heading out of town on another track. There had to be a reason that Jack didn't appear to be worried. We continued toward the train, and it toward us. The headlight looked as big as a washtub but I felt Jack knew what he was doing.

As we approached the motorcar setoff, Oklahoma Jack pulled the throttle back to stop and slammed the brake lever into the maximum stop position. We skidded to a stop perfectly at the motorcar setoff and as Jack dismounted the motorcar he shouted, "Set her off, Beck!" I slid out of my seat, grabbed the handles in the rear of the motorcar, picked up the rear of the car, spun the car around and with all my strength shoved the motorcar off the track. Within what seemed like only seconds, the train blew by us with the engine horns blowing continuously. You could smell the heat from the train brakes in emergency application as the first two thirds of the train rolled past us before coming to a stop.

I turned and looked at Jack just as he turned toward me. There was a completely different expression on his face, a look of relief. I said, "Damn, Jack!", and he just sat down shaking his head and said, "Yep, that was pretty close!" He then said something about my "doing a good job of keeping my head." I remember thinking that I really didn't realize until the last few seconds there was a reason to lose my head.

We had been given bad information by the train dispatcher. He had told us there would be no trains southbound for another hour and a half out of Purcell. He had overlooked the fact that this train had already left Purcell when we talked. Oklahoma Jack walked straight to a phone and called the train dispatcher and gave him one of the worst chewings, without using profanity, that I had ever heard. The dispatcher admitted his mistake, apologized and said that he had already turned himself in to the chief dispatcher.

I'm not sure what I learned that day. I know that if it hadn't been for Oklahoma Jack and the confidence that I had in him, there would have been a perfectly good motorcar destroyed that day because I would have abandoned ship pretty much as soon as I saw the headlight. Jack was a good man, and I used a lot of what he taught me for most of my years of service with the railroad.

RESPECT AND APPRECIATION

I had a accepted the position in the student foreman program, even though I had no intentions of making a career out of the railroad. It was a training position, so your time, as well as your soul, belonged to the roadmaster.

In a period of a couple of months, my roadmaster had moved me from one type of gang to another, letting me get a taste of several types of supervisory skills and responsibilities. Then something special happened to this unsuspecting young student foreman: The roadmaster assigned me to the mechanized tie gang to be an understudy on the most prestigious gang on the division. All other gang foremen on the division bid on and were awarded the foreman's job by seniority, but the tie gang foreman was appointed by division officers.

In those days, the tie gang was made up of fourteen or so large machines and operators, fifteen trackmen, two or three truck drivers, a foreman and his student foreman. As the name would suggest, the tie gang was charged with the renewal of crossties, the backbone of the railroad. At that time, this particular tie gang was renewing 500 to 750 ties a day. The system record for ties inserted in one day was around 1,000 ties, accomplished by a hot shot gang in California.

The foreman was a big man with a big voice as well as a big ego. He was a driving force as a boss. As the student foreman on the gang I was supposed to hone my supervisory skills by observing and assisting the foreman. My philosophy may have been a little different, or perhaps even a little strange to some. My thinking was that I needed to know the operation of the gang, its machines and its men before I could begin developing supervisory skills. I spent the first few weeks going from machine to machine, work station to work station observing, helping and when time permitted, actually operating the equipment.

In the beginning, the machine operators were a little leery of me and my habits, but I continued my methods. I would climb up on a machine and tell the operator to take a break and get a drink while I ran his machine for a few minutes. I would fall in with the trackmen when they would get behind and help them with their responsibilities. When the foreman would catch me doing my thing, he would voice his displeasure and point out that I was never going to make it as a foreman or a supervisor if I didn't change my ways and get to the business of supervising.

Early one morning at the depot, I was taking care of some of my assigned paperwork before the "on duty" time of the gang, when the roadmaster called me. He advised that the foreman was not going to be at work because of a sickness in his family, and that there was no other foreman available. He was going to be in a staff meeting all day and would not be available, either. He asked if I thought I could handle the gang for the day. I told him I could, even though I hadn't quite convinced myself of that fact. The roadmaster instructed me to just concentrate on safety and not worry about productivity, since the gang could get back on track the next day when the foreman returned.

I called all the men together and told them about the roadmaster's call. We had our morning safety discussion and I reminded the men that our main objective on that day was to work safely, watch out for each other and go home after work for the weekend to be with family and loved ones. I told them that despite the normal push for production and numbers, that was not my main concern nor should it be theirs. I emphasized that they were the best at what they do, for them to take care of their jobs and I would deal with the dispatchers, trains and the other day-to-day distractions.

As we prepared to go to work, one of the senior machine operators walked by me and said, "We're going to get you a thousand ties today." Before I could respond he was off and mounting his machine. At this point, the usual foreman would normally begin popping the figurative whip, hollering and yelling as if herding cattle out of the stock pens onto the range. However, this morning, as soon as I told the lead machines that we had authority from the dispatcher to enter the track and go to work, black smoke bellowed from the exhaust stacks and the roar of the diesel engines could be heard for miles as they headed out to the work location.

By the time I made it to the head end of the gang, they had already started pulling spikes and pushing the old ties from under the track. As I walked by the lead machine, another fellow worker walked by and said, "We are going to get you a thousand ties today!" I responded by saying that we didn't need to worry about numbers, we just needed to put in a good and safe day of work. Things were moving faster than I could ever remember seeing before. A little over an hour into the workday, the gang had already inserted 250 ties.

As I was walking toward the rear of the gang I noticed one of the machines was shut down. The machine operator advised that he had broken down. I told him I would call for a mechanic on the radio, as was customary, and that he could take a break until the mechanic arrived. The operator replied that he thought he could make the repairs in the time it would take the mechanic to arrive. I told him I appreciated the offer, but would go ahead and call the mechanic. About twenty minutes later the mechanic called to tell me the machine was up and running. I told him I appreciated his help. It turned out the machine was running when he arrived. The machine operator had made the repairs.

At lunchtime we had 750 ties inserted. It was the usual procedure to shut down the gang in sections and allow them to eat. I walked to the front end and told them to break for lunch. It turned out they had already eaten and the dust continued to fly. As I walked through the gang, I was amazed by how well everything was going. It really didn't seem like anyone was overexerting himself, but things seemed to be happening faster. Everyone was working in unison with pride, and the unusual thing was that most were smiling.

With about two hours left to work, we had inserted over 900 ties. That was about the time I received a call on the radio from the foreman. He had managed to take care of his family matters and was approaching the gang to finish the day. When he reached my location and found out the tie count, he was ecstatic. He began to walk the gang, hollering orders and instructions and yelling, "We're going to put one in the record books today!" The more he yelled, the slower the tie count climbed.

Everyone appeared to working as hard as they had earlier in the day, but the smiles were gone and productivity continued to drop. Then a machine broke down, and then another. The machine operators called the foreman on the radio and told him they were going to need a mechanic for repairs. The foreman called the train dispatcher and asked for an extension on our work time. The dispatcher asked, "What happened to Beck?"

The foreman told him not to worry about Beck, that he was now running the show. With that, the dispatcher told him, "Well, you and your show are going to have to clear the track. I've got trains to run."

With that being said, we cleared the track for the day. The gang had inserted 975 ties. As the foreman continued to throw a fit about how close he had come to a record day, I walked down through the gang telling them how much I appreciated their help, and what a fantastic job they had done. A dozen or more of the men responded quietly, "We could have gotten you over a thousand ties today."

Born that day was my philosophy, regarding not only management style, but day-to-day interactions with my fellow railroaders. I realized that respect and appreciation, along with the need to be firm but fair, could be the cornerstone of a successful career.

That was also the day I knew the railroad was what I wanted to be a part of for the rest of my working days.

Day to Day, Year to Year, Boy to Man

PART II

Adulthood, and the independence that came with it, were not working out as well as he had anticipated for so many years. It seemed that he was meandering through life being content with what the moment had to offer, rather than seeking a direction and making a plan. Teaching and coaching, at one time a driving force, had become more like a stroll on a foggy day. Then came a job opportunity with the Santa Fe Railroad. He didn't know anything about the railroad except the money was good. Even though he only lacked a few hours getting his degree, he had a new driving force, money, and he would never look back to the education that might have led him to a more than honorable profession.

The new job rekindled some of the drive and competitiveness that he had been missing for too long. He recognized the possibility of advancement and with that, more money. He worked long hours and traveled over several states. As a result of his efforts, promotions began to come.

READY OR NOT—FOREMAN BECK

By March of 1973 I had bounced around from location to location for almost a year working as a student foreman. I was becoming impatient as an ambitious twenty-three year old, and was beginning to lose interest in the training process. I felt ready to take the next step or even better, skip a step. I finally got to the point where I called the Division Engineer's Office and informed the chief clerk I was going to resign and go back to school, because I had apparently worked my way into a dead end.

He told me that was too bad, because he was just about to call me to tell me that I was being promoted to foreman, and that I was to report to Sweetwater, Texas to relieve the section foreman for an undetermined length of time. I swallowed a little pride and took the job as foreman. Thinking back, I was really fortunate to have the opportunity at twenty-three years of age to hold a position where the average age of the foremen working on my Division was about fifty-five years of age

I was confident but nervous as I reported to my first foreman's job. The good thing about working with a section gang was that, in most cases the older, more experienced men were on these gangs, and while I was proud and probably a little cocky, I did have enough sense to use their knowledge and experience to my advantage. It appeared that the regular foreman was going to be off work for at least a month, so I needed to get comfortable and make myself at home.

Everything went pretty well for the first few days. My first problem had to do with the paperwork and timekeeping involved in the job. Rather than call the main office and show my ignorance, I decided to call the regular foreman and ask him for a little assistance. I called his home and described the problems I was having. He told me I needed to talk to his wife. She got on the phone and proceeded to list everything that I needed to know and more. I asked how she had become so fluent in the paperwork. I was surprised to learn that she had been keeping her husband's books for twenty years. I later found out that when there was a foreman's meeting dealing with timekeeping or paperwork changes, this foreman would always bring his wife. She would sit in the class with him and take notes while he slept.

One night while working a derailment at the yard at Sweetwater, we were having trouble finding some of the material that we needed for repairs. I again called the regular foreman at home to find out if the material we needed was available. He again handed the phone to his wife and she told me where I could find each item I needed. Some were in Sweetwater, some in Lawn and some were in Coleman. She knew all the material names, slang names, sizes and how many were available.

On the morning of my fifth day on this job I received a note from the yardmaster concerning a yard switch that had been turned in by a switchman and reported as very hard to throw. I immediately loaded up the gang and repaired the switch so that it was then very easy to throw. That afternoon, upon returning to the yard office to tie up for the day, I was approached by the trainmaster who proceeded to verbally assault me because I had repaired a hard to throw switch and had not informed anyone of that fact. A switchman had injured himself by striking himself in the groin area with the switch handle. He apparently had expected the switch to be hard to throw and had jerked the switch handle toward him.

The trainmaster continued his attack on me for several more minutes until the roadmaster walked in and stepped between us. He put his finger in the trainmaster's face and began his own assault. He reminded the trainmaster that I did not work for him, and that if there was a problem he was to contact the roadmaster. He told the trainmaster that he would handle the situation with me. As he turned around I may have had a little smile on my face, but it went away quickly as I saw the seriousness of his glare. We walked outside, and he said, "Beck, get a damn haircut or put on a hair net! You look like a girl!", and then turned and walked off.

One early evening, I received a call in my hotel room concerning a derailment about ten miles east of Sweetwater. I called the men on the gang, and told them to meet me at the derailment site because there was no reason for them to come into town; I would go by the yard office, get the truck and meet them there. I arrived at the site and could see that there were several overturned rail cars. One of the cars was a refrigerated box car that contained Coors Beer, which was very popular, but at the time could not be purchased in Texas. I got out of the truck and walked over toward the car where there were cases of beer scattered all over the ground. All my men were already there, standing around like they were bird watching. I looked toward their personal vehicles parked nearby. The rear of each car was so low that the rear bumper was almost dragging the ground. I turned back toward my men. Not a one of them would make eye contact with me.

I saw the special agent of the Santa Fe Police walking around the beer car so I decided to see what he had on his mind. As I approached him, I noticed that he was putting several cases of Coors Beer in the trunk of his company vehicle. He looked up, saw me and told me that they were about to destroy all the beer that was involved in the derailment by running a bulldozer over it, crushing and burying it on our right-of-way. He told me he was taking some of the beer just in case they needed it for evidence.

I returned to my men and told them to move their cars further from the derailment site because they might get damaged so close to the site. We then worked several hours clearing and repairing the derailment site.

Coincidentally, three of the men on my gang called in sick the next morning.

It was probably something they ate.

LESSON LEARNED

A s a new foreman, one of my first gangs was a small gang made up of seven or eight men, all of whom had more time and experience than me. We were working on the San Angelo branch when a typical summer storm rolled up and it began to rain. There were some suggestions from the men that we head for cover and wait out the storm. Or, because we had already had a good productive day, and after all it was Friday, call it quits and go home. I assured them that a little rain wasn't going to melt them and that we were going to put in a full day.

About that time I saw a familiar white pickup truck bouncing down the old right-of- way road coming toward us. It was my roadmaster, "Big Boss." This was going to be good. I could already hear the "Atta-boy" coming my way for staying with the chore at hand, despite the weather. I walked down from the track to the road and stood there at semi-attention with rain dripping from the brim of my hardhat. He pulled right up next to me and rolled down his window about four inches and said "Beck, what the hell are you doing?"

I told him we were working and having one of our better production days. He replied "Don't you know it's raining?" I stammered around for a second, and said that I wasn't sure what his policy was concerning working in the rain. After which he replied "My policy is that the first drop of rain that hits you is by the Grace of God. The second drop of rain that hits you is your own damn fault!"

He then rolled up his window and drove off.

Lesson learned -- the first of many.

OKLAHOMA, 3.2 AND ME

Now that I was working as a gang foreman, I had three apartments in Texas, one each in Brownwood, Cleburne, and Dallas, so that I would always be working close to a place to stay. However, because I was the youngest foreman in age (24) and in seniority (1 year) I occasionally had to work in foreign countries, such as Purcell, Oklahoma.

I knew very little about Oklahoma, other than having taken part in the musical "Oklahoma" in high school, but I figured that wasn't going to help me with my Oklahoma etiquette. I did have an uncle that spent a lot of his younger days working in the Sooner State. My Uncle Allen was a mountain of a man who could tell a tale or two. When he found out I was going to Purcell to work, he felt obliged to give me some advice. He said, "Terry, I know good and well you are going to end up in a beer joint up there sooner or later, and you're going to find out that some of those folks don't have any use for fellers from Texas. So, you need to do what I always did; as soon as I walked into a bar, I would slam my fist down on a table and holler, 'I'm from Texas and proud of it, I want to know which one of you fellers is the meanest, baddest dude in this joint and I'm going to whip your butt, and then I don't want to be bothered by the rest of you fellers the rest of the time I'm in here.'"

Sure enough, my first night in beautiful downtown Purcell, Oklahoma, I decided that I wasn't going to sit in my motel room and stare at the walls so I drove down the street a ways and found a bar. It looked hospitable enough, as far as beer joints go, so I parked and walked in. The first thing that came to mind as I walked in was the advice that Uncle Allen had given me. As I stood just inside the door, I took a deep breath and looked around. There were a lot of dudes in there, and a bunch of them were on the large side. I took another deep breath and thought,

"Nah, there is no need to tell them I'm from Texas unless they ask."

Things went pretty well once I settled in. It didn't take long to figure out that a bar in Oklahoma was not much different than a bar in Texas. The folks were hospitable even after they found out I was from Texas (well, most of them were). I seemed to be handling my beer very well. I knew that work would come early the next morning so I didn't want to get carried away with the beer drinking. Then someone explained the thing about 3.2% beer in Oklahoma and I guess I let my guard down a little, since I cut my teeth on 6% Texas beer.

I finally decided I better head for the room, so I bid my new Oklahoma buddies farewell and walked outside to the sidewalk, reaching into my pocket for the truck keys. I was driving my little 1972 Chevrolet Luv pickup. As I looked toward my vehicle my heart stopped. The little white pickup was still there, but someone had stolen the tow-bar that was mounted on the front bumper, the tool box mounted in the bed, and the vinyl tarp covering the bed of the truck. I couldn't believe that some low-life had violated my pride and joy.

As I walked toward my little Chevy Luv, a Purcell police officer drove by. I flagged him down and told him of my dilemma. He was a young officer, about my age, and seemed very professional as he took my information. He asked me to describe in detail the items that were missing from my truck. I described the tow-bar, the tool box and the tarp. He seemed awful happy about the situation as he asked me to follow him. We walked about four vehicles down and then he stopped, pointed and said, "Did your stuff look a lot like this?"

A soberness settled over me as I realized that it was my truck, tow-bar and all. I now realized that there were at least two 1972 white Chevy Luv pickups in town, one with tow-bar, tarp and toolbox, and one without. The policeman then asked where I was staying. I pointed down the street a couple of blocks to the motel where I was registered. He suggested I walk down to my room and get some sleep. He asked me what time I would be getting up and around the next morning. I told him I would eat breakfast about 5:00 a.m. and be at work by 6:00 a.m. He said he would be on duty all night and would keep an eye on my little pickup. As I walked to my motel, all I could think was that I hoped the police officer didn't think I was as big an idiot as I felt like.

The next morning, as I walked out of the motel, there sat the police officer. As I walked toward him, he motioned for me to get into the patrol car. As I got in, he asked if I wanted to get a bite of breakfast. We ate breakfast in a little cafe where his wife worked. He introduced us and she said, "Oh, are you the guy with the little white pickup?"

We all laughed and visited, and soon the embarrassment from the night before faded. Although I didn't realize it then, I had been lucky again in several ways. Whether deserved or not, someone had watched over me, and even though I didn't learn my lesson then, they would look over me again and again until I finally learned that I was never alone, I was always loved, and that memories can teach, amuse, console and keep you company.

BUFFALO GAP DERAILMENT

In early 1973 I was foreman of the Sweetwater section gang. We had just finished a hard day's work in Lawn, Texas and were heading back to Sweetwater when we received a radio call from the train dispatcher. He had bad, mood changing news. There had just been a major train derailment at Buffalo Gap. We were to head that way immediately and give any assistance needed.

We were the first to reach the derailment site. We determined that the train crew was okay and that there was no hazardous material involved. There were twenty-five or thirty rail cars piled up in a relatively short space, looking like Pick Up Sticks. There was about a half a mile of main track either destroyed or heavily damaged, as well as the siding track. This was going to be a long, long process.

By dark, the work train had arrived at the site carrying the derrick crane, rail and crossties, ballast rock and most important, the derrick diner car. That first night, and well into the next day, the mechanical forces cleared the maze of derailed rail cars from the site by either picking them up with the derrick crane, or shoving and pulling them out of the way with huge dozers.

My gang and I spent all night running back and forth to Sweetwater and Brownwood, gathering additional track material that would be needed once the mechanical forces had cleared enough track for us to begin rebuilding the main track. It was determined that the siding would have to wait for another time. For now, all hands would work on getting train traffic moving on the main track.

We had just pulled back up to the derailment site as the sun began to peek over the somewhat smaller pile of wrecked rail cars. As we dismounted the section truck, the smell of bacon, eggs and coffee drifted heavily over the site. The cook, usually one of the older mechanical department men, began to ring the diner car bell which was an indication that he was ready to start the feeding process as time would permit. As we walked toward the site, the roadmaster hollered at me to go ahead and take my men to the diner before we started rebuilding the railroad.

For the next thirty or forty minutes, there wasn't a place on earth that we would have rather been. The old cook normally wasn't much to look at, but today deserved a big ol' hug. Eggs, ham, bacon, pancakes, biscuits, sausage, milk, coffee and orange juice for all. As we ate, the old cook was busy preparing grub for lunch. It was apparent that while we may get tired and need rest, if the cook had anything to do with it, we weren't going to be hungry.

As the day wore on, time began to take a toll as fatigue crept in. We began to take shifts going back to the truck and taking one or two hour naps. So went the night. By the next morning, the third day, we were finally laying the last rail and driving the last spikes as we connected up the main track. All that was left was to unload the ballast rock from the work train onto the track, jack the track up on top of the rock, and unload rock one final time. With fatigue being the biggest factor, this was going to be a tough few hours.

To unload ballast rock, it is necessary to walk alongside the train as it slowly moves at 1-2 MPH and operate the hopper doors with long heavy wrenches, letting the rock roll from the car onto the bare ties. Once started, you can't stop because the rock would pile up on the track and derail the car. As the rock rolled from the car, dust would rise up and stick to your sweaty face and arms, making visibility and breathing tough.

We had finished the first unloading, jacked and lined the track and were ready to start the final unloading of ballast rock. The roadmaster checked to see that we were all ready, then turned toward the engines and gave a hand signal to move the train ahead slowly. The train didn't move. He again gave the 'move ahead' signal and again the train didn't move. We looked toward the engines, about fifteen or so car lengths away, and we could see the engineer dismounting the locomotive and slowly walking toward us. The roadmaster grumbled, "What the hell is wrong with that engineer."

We all sat down on the edge of the track as we waited for the short stocky engineer to waddle down to our location. When he finally reached our location, he removed his hat, wiped the sweat from his brow and said, "Say Boss, I got to go home. My wife thinks she can't go into the bathroom and crap unless I'm there brushing my teeth, and I haven't been home in three days. Poor woman is in trouble." With that said he simply put his hat back on, turned and began his long walk back to the engine.

The roadmaster watched him walk a couple of car lengths and then turned toward us with a frown that melted away into a grin and finally into a full hearty laugh. We all sat there in the shade of the train laughing, and for a while forgot about the aching dominance of the fatigue that had long possessed our bodies. The old engineer finally got back to his engine and sounded two long blasts on his whistle which indicated he was ready to move ahead. We had a much needed break, as much mentally as physically, and with the sounding of the whistle, we stood and continued our trek toward completion of our formidable task.

LAKE LAVON LAUGHTER

One of my assignments in the early 1970s was serving as foreman on a track gang working out on the old Paris district. This was an old branch line that ran from North Dallas to Paris, Texas. My gang was involved with track construction in the Lake Lavon area. They were going to raise the water level in the lake, and it was necessary for the railroad to raise and reroute part of its track that ran near the watershed of the lake. We were reconstructing and raising several miles of railroad track.

One of the more time consuming parts of this project was building up the roadbed on which the track ran. To build up the roadbed, we had to haul tons of rock, dirt and gravel out to the work site on a work train, and dump it from special train cars. Then heavy equipment would shove and move the material, and start building the roadbed higher. These special railroad cars were called air dump cars. They work a lot like the dump bed of a dump truck. Each has to be dumped, one car at a time. The cars operate off the compressed air that runs through the train from the locomotives. In order to dump the tons of material in each car, it is necessary to manipulate several valves, and then huge cylinders push one side of the car upward, just like a dump truck. As the tons of material start to slide toward the low side of the car, the car side hinges downward allowing the material to slide out of the car and onto the ground alongside the track.

The work train would usually have the same train crew on it day after day. As foreman, I was responsible for seeing that the job was done, and the conductor on the work train was supposed to be responsible for the movements of the train. Ideally, the conductor would be on the ground standing next to me, where I would inform him of the necessary instructions about train movements, and he would then relay the information to his crew. However, this particular conductor had his own ideas as to what his responsibilities were. He spent most of his time sitting in the caboose while his brakeman stood with me doing the conductor's job.

One day the work train arrived out on the job site. As usual, I spoke to the conductor and told him what the work plan was for that day. He instructed his brakeman to take care of it and said that if we needed him, he would be on the caboose doing paperwork. I reminded the conductor, again, that he should be with us on the ground helping with the work at hand and that he should uncouple the caboose from the air dump cars and leave it sitting clear of the work area for safety's sake. He once again informed me that I should take care of my business, and that he would manage his business. He said that the caboose would remain coupled to the work train so that he would be near the work area. With that being said, we began the task of dumping the twenty-five air dump cars.

Everything was proceeding as usual and we were down to dumping the last air dump car which, as the last car in the train, was coupled into the caboose. As we began the dumping process and one side of the car began to rise, the tons of material in the car seemed to stick to the bottom of the car, instead of sliding toward the low side of the car. There was apparently a mechanical problem with the lower side of the car. It didn't hinge downward and when the material finally let go, it came down with such a heavy force on the lower side of the car that it turned the car over. When the car turned over it also turned the caboose over, being that it was still coupled to it.

We all ran to rear of the caboose yelling the conductor's name, fearful of what we might find. About the time we arrived at the rear of the caboose, which was lying on its side, the conductor came crawling out of the door. It was a horrible sight. His eyes were as big as saucers and he was covered from head to toe with waste from the toilet. He was apparently catching up on some reading while sitting on the caboose toilet when his world was turned upside down. Fortunately he was not seriously injured.

When we got ready to head in, the conductor asked if he could ride with us in a vehicle. I told him there was no way he was getting in any of my vehicles. Besides, he needed to stay with his train crew. As he boarded the locomotive and tried to enter for the long ride back to town, he was unable to enter because the crew had locked him out. They made him ride on the outside of the locomotive all the way back to town.

I'm sure that there were several valuable lessons learned that day, but not necessarily by the right person. However, he did pick up several new nicknames, and most were best not voiced in public.

In the end, it seemed the incident only enhanced his "crappy" attitude.

ALL ABOARD!
LEAVING LAWN, READY OR NOT!

It really wasn't all that bad once I became used to the routine. I never had been much of an early morning person, but I hadn't been a railroader for all that long, either. It had been long enough for me to have learned that time, or more specifically, night and day, were not defined as they once were. It was nothing to get up and be on the road at three or four o'clock in the morning to get to a job that started at six in the morning, just so I could spend a few hours at home rather than within the confines of a four walled motel room. That's the reason I was on the road this young Fall morning, heading down a lonely highway to my very own Santa Fe extra gang headquartered in Lawn, Texas.

I pulled up next to the house track in Lawn and was pleased to see the gang's outfit cars had been moved from Coleman, as I had requested over the weekend. There were two bunk cars, a water car, a fuel car and a boxcar for tools and supplies. None of the men had stayed in the cars over the weekend, but they were already there this morning, getting the cars set up for occupation and carrying their personal belongings inside. As I stepped out of my pickup, I could see smoke coming from the stack of one of the bunk cars, and could smell the tantalizing aroma of bacon, eggs and coffee. Then old Bob stuck his head out the bunk car door and hollered, "Hey Boss, I got plenty of breakfast ready. Come on in and get a bite!"

"No thank you, Bob. Y'all go ahead and eat. I stopped and got something on the way", I hollered back. I had stopped and bought a Pepsi and a Baby Ruth and the fresh smell of breakfast was killing me, but I had things to do before we went to work in about thirty minutes. I had a small gang with two machine operators, one truck driver, and four trackmen. They were a good gang with a mixture of older experienced men, young strong go-getters not afraid of hard work, and a couple of cut-ups to keep the job fun. Jake, the oldest man on the gang, was more or less my lead man because he lived in the area, had the most experience, was very familiar with the people and towns in the area and, well, he was old. Jake's claim to fame was that he was the Mayor of Buffalo Gap, Texas, although most didn't think there was a lot of truth in his claim.

It was about 0555. I had finished my paperwork and talked to the train dispatcher about our work location for the day when I glanced toward the bunk cars, and saw the men slowly descending the stairs with their grips and lunch buckets in hand. They sauntered over to my location, found a place to sit, and finished lacing their boots as I began our Monday morning safety meeting. I finished the meeting by telling the men we were going to be working toward Buffalo Gap that day, changing out cross ties. I told Jake to take the truck and men to the location and start the prep work, and the machine operators and I would travel by rail and meet them at the work location.

As the two machine operators and I prepared the machines for rail travel, Alex, one of the operators, asked if he could take a couple of hours off when it was convenient, so he could travel into Abilene and take care of some personal business. Alex was an excellent machine operator, hard working and a good man. He never missed work so I knew if he was asking off, especially with no advanced notice, it must be important to him or his family. I told him if it was important to him, he could take care of that business now, and just meet us at the job site when he was finished. I would operate his machine until he returned. Alex shook my hand, said thank you, and told me to just dock his time for the morning even though he had put in almost an hour of work. I told him not to worry about it, that we would work it out later.

The other machine operator and I powered up the machines and began our five mile journey to the work site via the rail. I wouldn't have admitted it to Alex, but another reason I let him go so easily was because I loved operating his machine. I loved traveling on the rail through areas no other mode of transportation could access, seeing nature at its undisturbed best, crossing streams and rolling through valleys cut through the sides of hills, exposing multicolored rocks and formations thousands, or even millions, of years old. Around every curve lay something new or unexpected: Perhaps an old metal wheeled tractor sitting among the mesquite trees bearing the scars of age, hard work and the perils of nature and time, or an old Model A automobile, now barely recognizable, making you wonder how and why the old car ended up here, somehow still looking like that's where it belonged. Or you might stop to let a mother Bobcat hurriedly help her three kittens over each rail and quickly vanish in the Johnson grass wall at the edge of the track. It was always a refreshing journey, especially in the early morning just as the sun crawled over the tops of the West Texas hills.

We approached the work site and sounded the horns on the machines to alert the men, already hard at work, of our approach. They had already gotten off to a good start, so as soon as we rolled up we prepared the machines for work mode and the dust started flying. The men knew my philosophy was to get the hard work out of the way early in the coolness of the morning and save the easy stuff or any occasional 'goofing off' for later, in the heat of the day. I had told the men in our morning meeting that our goal was to replace fifty cross ties by lunch. Then we would spend the afternoon cleaning up and dressing the work area before hauling the old ties back to Lawn.

We had been working about an hour when an old gentleman walked up to the track. I was still operating the machine and motioned to the man to stay where he was, thinking he wanted to talk to me. However, he waved to Jake, who walked over to him, escorted him back out of the work area and began talking to him. About that time Alex arrived at the job site and relieved me on his machine. I walked over to Jake and the other man, and Jake introduced him to me. He was one of Jake's fellow Buffalo Gap residents and he was asking if he could buy some of the old ties that we were removing from the track.

It was always funny back in the old days; We could be in the middle of nowhere, not see a soul anywhere for hours, and then pull a couple of old ties out of the track and within fifteen minutes an old rancher would be standing there, wanting to know if he could have the ties for fence corner posts. Back then, the roadmaster had control over handling used or scrap ties, and my roadmaster had told me that all old cross ties we removed were mine if I wanted them, to dispose of as I wished, as long as I kept the right-of-way clean and clear of old ties.

I asked the old fellow how many ties he would need, and what he would be using them for. He said that they wanted to use them for several landscaping projects back in Buffalo Gap involving a church, the steak house and several other buildings. How many they needed would depend on the cost. I told him that I would give them all to him free of charge, but they would have to take all the scrap ties, as well as the usable ones, in order to clean the right-of-way. He practically shook my arm off thanking me, and said he would be back in the early afternoon with a truck and some help to load the ties. I told him that I would move the ties to the edge of Railroad property, and asked them to limit their time on Railroad property. He was still waving and thanking me when he got in his pickup.

The gang and I finished up the job and stacked the ties next to the right-of-way road. We were loading up our tools and equipment when the man from Buffalo Gap drove up in an old stake bed truck. He and another older gentleman got out of the truck and began to load the ties. I don't think they had realized how heavy an old water soaked cross tie could be. I watched them load the first tie and couldn't stand it any longer. I hollered at the men and told them to grab a couple of sets of tie tongs off the truck and load these ties for the gentlemen right quick. The men grabbed their tools and made short work of loading the ties, making it look easy because it was something they did every day. Plus, they liked to show off when they had a chance.

The two old men thanked us and thanked us until I finally escorted them to their truck. I asked if they were going to have help unloading the ties. They said that they weren't sure. I turned to my men and told them to head back into Lawn and tie up for the day and I was going to follow the men back into Buffalo Gap and help them unload the ties. Alex said he could meet us there and help, as did Jake and Bob. I told them that I appreciated the offer, but that I could not pay them after-hours time for work not connected with the railroad. The three of them said that was fine with them, and that they didn't mind helping. I instructed the remaining men to head back into Lawn, and told them I would come by there later to do my paperwork.

With all that being said, we headed for Buffalo Gap. We wound our way through the beautiful countryside until we finally ended up in downtown Buffalo Gap, population around 300. We parked and walked back to the rear of the truck to begin the task of unloading the ties. To my surprise, my complete gang pulled up and without saying a word, went to work. In nothing flat, they unloaded the ties into a nice neat stack. As we were about to leave, Jake walked up to me and said that his fellow Buffalo Gap folks wanted to treat us to supper for the work we had done for them. I told him that I appreciated it, but that I was heading back to Brownwood as soon as I finished my paperwork. He and the rest of the men could certainly take them up on the offer, however. The men very happily accepted the invitation, and were told to be back at the steakhouse about 6:30 p.m. With that, we said goodbye and headed back to Lawn.

Back in Lawn, I finished my paperwork, sent my daily work wires and stopped back by the bunk cars. I stuck my head inside the door, hollered that I was leaving and instructed the men to try not to embarrass the railroad at the appreciation supper. Alex, Bob and a couple of the other fellers came over to my truck as I was getting in, and said that they would feel more comfortable if I would join them at the supper. I told them I appreciated it, but I just didn't want to drive back to Brownwood that late. They then argued that I should stay in the bunk car with them since they had an extra bunk. I finally gave in; After all, I did always carry a bag with several changes of clothes, so it would work.

We all cleaned up and put on our 'going to town' clothes and headed to Buffalo Gap, not really knowing what to expect. We met Jake and his lovely wife there at the steakhouse. There were sure a lot of cars already parked around the building, but it wasn't surprising, in that this steakhouse was well known for miles around. People would come all the way from Abilene, Brownwood, Sweetwater and San Angelo just to eat their steak. Jake had told us we were to just come on in when we got there, and there would be a table reserved for us. I looked around at the men. It struck me that these old railroaders cleaned up pretty good, and I motioned for them to go ahead. They in turn said I should go first, and they would follow. I shrugged, opened the door and in we went. As we entered the door, most everyone in the restaurant stood and started clapping. We stopped, and for a second looked like a herd of sheep fixing to stampede. Then after the shock was over, we sauntered over to our table and sat down. As we all sat down, I felt kind of proud to be with these guys.

We sat there, and ate and ate and ate. It was delicious. After we had eaten about all we could hold, someone at the next table stood up to say they appreciated our efforts, and while they didn't have much money in the city budget, they did have damn good food. Then he said that the Mayor would like to say a few words. I think every gang member's mouth fell open when old Jake stood up and said a few words. It was amazing. He didn't cuss, didn't have a chew in his mouth, and you could actually understand what he was saying. After Jake's "State of Buffalo Gap" speech, we were invited to go over to the barbeque restaurant and saloon for all the beer we could drink and all the pool we could shoot, all on the house. I don't know what made them think that a bunch of railroaders, and I must say "well dressed railroaders", would drink beer or shoot pool, but to keep from hurting anyone's feelings we went to the barbeque place.

As we strolled down the street to the barbeque/saloon I held a little safety meeting. I told the men that we were off duty and I couldn't tell them what to do, but I suggested that we were still representing the proud Santa Fe railroad and we should handle ourselves in such a manner as not to bring embarrassment to our company. Bob spoke up and said, "Yes Daddy, we will behave!" Then he pointed out that at 24, I was the youngest on the gang by nearly ten years and that they would keep an eye on me.

We had a blast drinking a few beers and shooting pool with some of the locals. There was shuffleboard, foosball and pinball galore. I saw a side of my men that I had never seen before, and it felt good. I suppose they also saw a side of me that they hadn't seen out on the railroad right-of-way, and I hoped that it was good. We made new friends that night. We shared railroad stories, ranching and farming happenings, and toward the end we got around to the good old beer drinking stories. The goodbyes took a while but we finally gathered ourselves up, and headed back to Lawn and the comfort of the bunk cars. It had been a good day, and it had been a really good night.

We arrived back at Lawn and wasted little time hitting the bunk, knowing 5:00 a.m. was going to be coming along before long. The men were all in one bunk car, while I would have a bunk car all to myself. Having never spent the night in a bunk car before, I was having a little trouble sleeping. One adjustment I was having difficulty with was that every time a train ran down the main line I could feel the bunk car rock and vibrate, in that we were only a few feet from the main line and the trains blowing by at about 50 MPH or so. About 4:00 a.m. another train rolled down the main, waking me as the bunk seemed to do a little rock and roll. After the train had gone by, I lay there, still half asleep, and realized I still felt a moving sensation. I lay there a few seconds and then sat up, raised the window shade and peeked out the window just in time to see a telephone pole slowly pass by...CRAP!!!!! WE WERE MOVING!

I bailed from my bunk and ran to the door. As I opened the door, which was about four feet above the ground, I could see the bunk car steps, chained to the side of the car, slowly dragging below the door. Barefoot and dressed in a pair of my best Fruit of the Looms, I jumped from the door and started placing some old pieces of lumber under the rolling wheels in an effort to stop the slowly rolling cars. The wheels were crushing the old wood as fast as I shoved it on the rail. I ran to the boxcar, climbed the ladder to the top of the car and set the handbrake, finally bringing the five cars to a slow stop. I stood on the side of the boxcar for a minute waiting for my heart to slow down and to catch my breath, then hobbled back to the bunk. It had seemed like the cars had rolled forever, but in reality they had only rolled about fifty yards. If they had rolled another hundred yards, they would have been on the main track and I shuddered to think of all the possibilities. I shuddered again when it hit me: I wasn't even supposed to be there, and what if I hadn't been?

Back in the bunk, I cleaned the blood from the bottom of my feet and removed as many stickers and splinters as I could stand before getting dressed and walking back outside to assess the damage, finish securing the cars and find the reason the cars had moved. Fortunately, there was no damage. It also became obvious that the cars had not been properly secured. About that time, Bob opened the bunk car door, looked down at me, looked back at our vehicles parked about fifty yards from the bunk car and hollered, "Hey, who moved my pickup and the other vehicles?"

I told him that the vehicles had not moved. He then looked back to the vehicles, then toward the main line switch, then back at me and said, "Oh crap! We'll be out there in a minute, Boss!"

Someone hadn't done their job, nor had I. We were going to have a talk about it. We were going to come to an understanding. This would never happen again.

In twenty-four hours I had seen, done, and absorbed more than I had ever expected while driving down that lonely West Texas highway that early Fall morning. There were lessons learned, new friends made, good deeds done, rewards shared, and responsibilities recognized in this third year of my railroad adventure.

IT TAKES ALL KINDS

I spent some time as foreman of a large construction gang rebuilding the tracks in the shop area of Cleburne yard. This was not one of the most popular gangs on the division, due to the fact it was a headquartered gang that did not pay living expenses, and because there was a lot of hard work involved. Because of this, the gang was comprised mostly of young new-hires.

One day, several of the new-hires were eating lunch together in the shade of one of the shop buildings. What they did not know was that I was just a few feet from them around the corner of the building, and could hear every word they said. Apparently they had heard about a fellow employee that had been injured and had just made a sizeable settlement with the company.

One of the new employees, whom I will call "John", asked one of the other men, "If I were to get my hand cut off out here on the job, how much money do you think I would get?"

The other employee said, "I don't know, John. Maybe four or five thousand dollars."

Then John said, "Well, how much do you reckon I would get if I just got one finger cut off?"

"Probably two or three thousand dollars, I guess." said the other fellow.

John paused for a while and then said, "Well then, I guess it would be better if I lost my hand one finger at a time, wouldn't it?"

New-hires had a sixty-day probation period after going to work before they were officially hired as a full time employee. During these sixty days, they were not union members and could be released from employment for a variety of reasons. I saw to it that John's railroad career was a total of six days long, which in my opinion was five days too many.

I'VE GOTTEN OVER IT

There's something that's bothered me for many years. I never really felt comfortable discussing it with others, especially in my younger days. Now, a little older and hopefully a little wiser, I have found that problems often have a way of getting better if shared with friends or family. It is for that reason I have finally decided to share something that I have carried around with me for years, gnawing at my soul, weighing me down and possibly preventing me from fully enjoying life as it was meant to be.

It was the Fall of 1976 when this personal affliction nearly did me in. I was a young track gang foreman working in the huge mechanical shops in Cleburne, Texas. I was in charge of a twenty-five man gang rebuilding the trackage within these shops. We had been working in the shops for quite some time, and had become familiar with both the facility and its personnel. At the time, my wife Amber and I were living in Cleburne, her home town. This made the job a little more attractive in that I could be home in ten minutes or less, occasionally run home for lunch, and most importantly, enjoy the privacy of my home bathroom facilities when necessary.

This is where I probably ought to do a little explaining about my problem: Modesty. You see, I had always been a modest person. Even at home with four brothers, my dad and my poor mom, I was a nervous wreck because we only had one bathroom with no lock on the door. It was in this room I learned to sing and sing loud. Public bathroom facilities with multiple stalls became a nightmare for me.

On this particular day, I had been battling the effects of a stomach virus. I had fought through most of the day, hoping to make it to quitting time and the privacy of my own bathroom. Suddenly the effects of the virus took a turn for the worse and it was evident I wasn't going to make it home.

On this fine day in Cleburne, Texas it became obvious to me that I was going to have to use the shop bathroom facility. This may be the day I developed high blood pressure. I walked into the facility. It wasn't very wide, but it was very long. Along one side of the room were about twenty stalls, separated by partitions that started about a foot off the floor and extended up only about two feet or so with no doors in front. I really didn't have time to critique the facilities any further, but noticed one thing in my favor; there was no one else in the room. If I took care of my business quickly, I could be out before anyone else came in.

I rushed as rapidly as I could safely do so to the last stall in the room. I had no more than made myself comfortable (probably not the correct word) when I heard the door squeak and in walked one of the shop laborers. There I sat with my head sticking up above the partition, like a chicken on a nest. He had no more than entered the room when he looked my way and hollered, "Hey Beck, what's goin' on?"

I looked down at the floor and answered, "Aw, not much," hoping this would be a quick visit on his part. But no - he just kept walking in my direction, talking a mile a minute, although I really wasn't concentrating on what he was saying. Before he made it all the way to me, the door squeaked again, and he turned to the person walking in.

"Hey Joe!" he hollered, "Looky here, here's ol' Beck! You can ask him yourself about that next track they are building."

The second dude starts walking my way, just a-talkin' up a storm. They both walk down to the entrance to my stall, prop up their feet, and make themselves comfortable. Then the door squeaks again. And again. Several others come into the room and proceed to walk down my way and join in on the conversation (a conversation in which I had not uttered over two words). My thoughts at the time were, "Doesn't anybody come in here to actually use the bathroom?"

That was the day I found out where all the laborers go to hide out from their bosses. I sat there for what seemed like hours with beads of sweat building on my forehead, trying not to make eye contact with anyone.

I sat there like the centerpiece on a conference table. I sat there so long that my legs fell asleep.

I had almost reached the point where I was going to yell some profane words of warning when the door squeaked again, someone poked their head in and yelled, "The boss is comin'!" and they scattered like a covey of quail.

At last, a little privacy. I wiped the sweat from my brow, bowed my head and, if I still could, was about to finish my business when the door squeaked. Crap! In walked the shop boss. He proceeded to walk all the way down to my nest, puffing on his cigar like a steam engine. "Hey Beck, what's goin' on?" He went on and on and on about how he had to come into the restroom every once in a while just to keep his men from hiding out. I just sat there with tears in my eyes, wondering if anybody in this whole damn shop ever came into that room just to use it for what it was designed for and just leave.

I finally left that room, not really sure if I would ever poop again. Since that time, considering all the surgeries and hospitalizations I've had, more people have probably seen me naked than Gypsy Rose Lee, so my modesty is mostly just a memory now.

Age changes a lot of things, including writing a silly story like this and sharing it with tens of people....one or two of them probably women.

CITY BOY?

It was a beautiful spring morning as I hy-railed down the track in the piney woods of East Texas on the Santa Fe's Longview district. I would be patrolling track as a track supervisor for the next two weeks between St. Augustine and Longview, Texas. It was an enjoyable job because the track was in pretty good shape, the train traffic was not that heavy and the scenery was beautiful. The stress level is a lot less when you're not dodging a train every few miles. You are able to make the necessary inspections and still take time to enjoy the natural beauty of that area.

It was my third day on this particular job, and it had been pretty uneventful. As I hy-railed just north of Beckville, I came upon a rather large pine tree that had fallen across the track. I checked with the dispatcher and determined there wouldn't be a train for a couple of hours. Therefore, I would have time to remove the tree myself. A chainsaw was a vital part of that job. After about forty-five minutes or so I had cut the tree in small enough pieces to remove them from the track and was on my way again.

I had only gone about half of a mile when I came upon animal remains scattered across the track. It wasn't a pretty sight. It was almost as if the large animal had exploded into small pieces. I got out of my hy-rail truck, began to walk the area and figured out it had been a cow. As I continued my inspection, trying to find a brand or ear tag in order to identify the owner, a man crossed over the right-of-way fence and approached me.

"When am I going to get paid for my two cows?" he asked. I told him that I thought that there was only one cow involved. He then said, "No, two cows. See, there is one heart here and another heart over there—two hearts, two cows. You city boys don't know much about cattle."

I responded, "Well, I see only one cow. See there are only four hooves: one, two, three, four. Even in the city, four hooves usually indicate one cow."

He smiled briefly and said, "Well, when am I going to get paid for my prize cow? Poor thing was like a member of the family."

So, that is how the first half of my third day on this assignment went, and the railroad education process continued for this "city boy."

YOU MIGHT GET WHAT YOU ASK FOR

Years back, the old Santa Fe railroad had a depot or station every ten miles or so, and assigned to each depot would be an agent. These agents were in charge of a variety of activities and personnel. Usually there would be a section gang, signalman and sometimes a switch crew or local train crew. The agent would also handle freight delivered at his location and deal with customers. Usually there would be stock pens on the property. The old depot agent was known by one and all.

One such depot and agent was located in Bangs, Texas, about 10 miles west of Brownwood. This old agent was all powerful. Well, maybe not all powerful, but in his mind he was "the man." There was a problem developing in Bangs that concerned the delivery of freight. It seems that westbound trains (running from Brownwood to Sweetwater) with freight to deliver to Bangs at night would not always stop the train before delivering the freight. They would simply throw said freight from the train to the loading dock as they rolled through Bangs. The reason for this act was due to the fact that these westbound trains had to pull up one of the steepest grades on the territory, Bangs Hill. If they stopped their train at Bangs and they were on a heavy train, it was very difficult for even the most experienced engineer to get his train moving again after the delivery was made.

The agent became furious about this practice and put out a bulletin stating that in the future all trains that had a delivery to Bangs at night would stop their train and deliver the freight inside the depot, without fail. Those failing to follow these instructions would be reported and disciplined.

The next night there was a train with a delivery for Bangs and they followed the agent's instructions to the letter. Everything was delivered inside the depot and the doors locked. The next morning the agent arrived and as he walked to the depot, a smile came on his face as there was no freight scattered on the dock. As he unlocked the door and entered, there they were: fifty head of goats making themselves at home.

There was no longer a smile on the old depot agent's face.

THE SECRET OF THE WASHITA AND ME

At twenty-five, I was foreman on a steel gang. A steel gang was a high priority gang with some of the most talented and specialized personnel in the engineering department. I was honored to be given the opportunity, especially at such a young age, and with less than a year's experience as a foreman.

We were working on the main line track between Davis and Dougherty, Oklahoma. This portion of track follows the Washita River as it cuts its way through the beautiful Arbuckle Mountains. The scenery was sometimes a distraction from the work at hand. About twenty to thirty feet from one side of the track were the steep walls of the Arbuckles and on the other side, within only a few feet, was the drop off into the Washita River. The river and track looked like a giant snake winding its way through the 350 foot granite walls that run for about fifteen miles through this area.

We were changing out the old rail, which has a tendency to wear out as trains 5000 - 7500 feet long traversed around the curves. The old rail was replaced with new strands of rail, each ¼ mile long, which weighed 119 pounds every three feet. We would begin work every morning at 6 a.m. and shut down by 2 p.m. in an effort to avoid the heat of the day.

After several weeks, we were finishing up with the last strand of rail and had plans to let the gang go early, in order to prepare for the move to the next work location. We had cleared the main track and were in the process of preparing the work equipment for moving, when the first train passed us moving southbound. Within several minutes of it having passed us we heard the train transmit on the radio, "Emergency, emergency, emergency! Our train has derailed!"

The train had derailed several hundred feet prior to the new rail we had just finished laying, but before the train came to a stop, several hundred feet of the freshly laid rail had been damaged. There were several hopper cars, once loaded with corn, derailed and leaning on their sides against the steep granite wall. Two of the cars had been ripped open and corn was covering the ground and track. It was necessary to walk through corn up to your waist to inspect the damage. It was determined that the derailment was caused by one of the hopper cars leaking out most of the corn on one side of the car, causing it to become unbalanced, so that as it entered the curve it leaned and its wheels left the rail, derailing the car.

After several hours, the train, the derailed cars and the corn were finally cleared so that we could begin making repairs to the track. It was terribly hot and humid as we worked well into the night, repairing the track and once again relaying the damaged rail. After finishing the repairs and opening the track for trains, the roadmaster felt it would be necessary for the track to be walked and inspected after each train through the remainder of the night. I volunteered for the job. I knew it was a tough job, but the pay was good.

After everyone left, I built a campfire not far from the track and waited for the first train. The first train rolled by slowly, after which I walked the track. I returned to the campfire and tried to get comfortable, because I knew from talking to the dispatcher earlier that it was going to be over an hour before the next train. As I sat there tired and miserably dirty, all I could think of was how great a cool refreshing shower would be. Then I became aware of the sounds of the river as it rolled by just fifty feet away. I began to think how nice it would be to wash a couple of layers of dirt and dried sweat off, not to mention the fact that it would recharge me and make the remainder of the night more tolerable. After all, I did have my suitcase in the truck with a nice clean change of clothes.

That's when I decided to disrobe and take a needed bath in the cool waters of the Washita River. I think I have pointed this out to some of you previously, but this is just another example of the fact that sometimes 'smart' and I don't get along. Anyway, I carefully climbed down the steep bank toward the rolling river. As I reached the water's edge, I sat my railroad lantern down on a nearby rock and looked into the water.

I knew the water was moving with some force but figured I would just ease down into the water and hang onto the rocky bank.

As I eased down toward the water, the rock I was standing on dislodged and sent me tumbling into the river. Before I could react, I had washed fifty feet or so down river. I finally got upright and could feel the bottom with my feet, but the force of the water was more than I could handle as I continued my trip down river. The only chance I had was to try and get close enough to the bank to grab hold of something. Finally, I was able to grab hold of an old log that had become lodged into the bank. For the first time I was able to look back and try to spot my lantern--I couldn't see it. The bank was too steep for me to try to climb. I knew I didn't want to take a chance and go further down stream, so I began to work my way back upstream by holding on to rocks, logs and briers.

After about thirty minutes I could finally see the lantern -- It looked like it was a mile away. I began to get extremely tired and would periodically stop to find a location where I could wedge myself between boulders in order to rest my arms. Still, the bank was too steep to climb up so I continued upstream. Finally, I reached the lantern, but had to wait a few minutes because I was too weak to pull myself out of the water. Just as I pulled myself up on the bank, the next train slowly approached. I decided that my best bet was to lie between the rocks until the train passed. I didn't think I wanted to explain my nakedness to a bunch of talkative railroaders.

The train seemed to take forever to pass, but I was finally able to climb up to the track, walk a short distance to my truck, tend to the cuts and scrapes that I could reach, and at last put on a clean, dry set of clothes. I walked the track and made my inspection and returned to my smoldering campfire.

I sat down, leaned back and took a deep breath as I looked up to see the slight glow beginning to appear in the eastern sky behind the silhouette of the Arbuckle Mountains. Life felt good. This was an amazing night. I was a lucky man. As I sat there, I made the decision that it would be a long time before anyone would know about the events of that night.

Thirty-six years is probably long enough.

Day to Day, Year to Year, Boy to Man

PART III

———————◆———————

All was looking good on the work front. However, his social life was suffering. There were good times along the way, but they would come to an end with a splash of cold water in the face the next morning, with the only reminder of the night before being his aching head and bloodshot eyes. And so it went for what seemed like forever. Work, work, work—anything to delay the loneliness of his personal time.

Then one night, despite all his apparent efforts to avoid it, he met an unbelievable woman who would eventually change his life and make him whole. There had been other good women along the way, but for whatever the reasons, he had always been able to run them off. It still took several years, but there was finally a wedding that sealed the relationship that had grown from acquaintance, to friend, to best friend, to wife AND best friend.

JUST ANOTHER DAY IN THE LIFE
OF A RAILROADER AND HIS FAMILY

Amber and I have been looking through and sorting old photos, clippings and various memorabilia again and came across an old picture. It wasn't a very clear photo, but it instantly brought memories bouncing around the room as Amber and I reminisced.

It was June of 1976 and Amber and I had only been married for four months. It was a Sunday and, as with most Sundays, we were at Amber's mother and dad's house having lunch in Cleburne, Texas. I had brought my pickup because I had plans to leave from there and travel to Silsbee, Texas to relieve on a track supervisor's position for a few weeks.

After finishing lunch, my father-in-law, Bud McPherson, a long time conductor with the Santa Fe, put on his conductor's uniform and prepared to go to work on the northbound Amtrak passenger train leaving Cleburne that afternoon. I told him I was getting ready to leave town, and offered to drop him off at the depot so he wouldn't have to leave his truck sitting there.

He agreed, and we were off to the depot. I stood around the depot talking to Bud and several other railroaders I knew and then watched Bud get on the train. After the train departed, I stood there talking to the agent for a few more minutes, when on the radio came an emergency broadcast. The passenger train had struck a semi truck loaded with rebar in Joshua, Texas (just a few miles north of Cleburne) and had derailed the locomotives and all but one of the passenger cars. I called Amber, informed her of the incident, and told her I was heading to the derailment site and would let her and the family know something as soon as I could.

I arrived at the scene within minutes, and one of the first things I saw was Bud walking from car to car, helping passengers evacuate. I put on my boots and hardhat and joined him, helping all that I could. Bud made me proud. The way he had taken control and kept everything as organized as possible until more help arrived proved he was a railroader's railroader.

Within just a few more minutes, Amber and her family drove up to the derailment site. Bud walked over to the cars, told everyone he was okay, to their relief, and went back to work. Because I was the first of my department at the scene, I began to evaluate the damage and list all the materials that would be needed, along with estimates as to how long it would take to get the track back in service, and communicated all this info via the radio to the chief dispatcher. Within an hour, the railroad workforce, supervision and other trained personnel began to arrive and as soon as I updated the supervisor who would be in control on all my information, I asked if I could be released to begin my four hour trip to Silsbee, Texas to be available for my relief job at 6 a.m. the next morning.

Yep, just another day in the life of a railroader and his family.

THE TRINITY RIVER INCIDENT

In 1976 I was busy working Relief track supervisor jobs through most of the summer, on account of it being prime vacation time. One of the relief jobs was covering for a track supervisor whose territory ran from Cleburne, Texas through Dallas to Denton, Texas, covering about one hundred and ten miles of track. It was a particularly difficult territory, even for a more experienced person, due to the hundreds of switches to inspect, grade road crossings to cross and inspect without getting hit by road traffic, a large number of industrial tracks, and dodging numerous trains and switchers.

Almost every day was an adventure. There wasn't much telling what you were going to find or see on or near the right-of-way. In addition to the normal track-related stuff, you could find abandoned automobiles (mostly stolen and stripped), dead animals of every type, and hobos and homeless people living in makeshift homes on or near the railroad property. You could also see the most beautiful and touching sights on any given day, such as wild animals caring for their young, quiet little streams and majestic trees and vegetation of many types.

On this particular day there had been heavy rains in the area, so I was paying particular attention to the bridges, rivers and streams, looking for potential problems such as washouts and driftwood fouling bridges. I was hy-railing the track from Cleburne toward Dallas when I reached the Trinity River bridge on the west side of Dallas. This bridge was long, over a thousand feet, and very high. I hy-railed very slowly across the bridge, stopping every hundred feet or so to inspect the driftwood build-up below.

During one of these stops I looked down, and a chill ran through my body as I saw what appeared to be a body twisted in the mass of drift-wood below. A little case of panic began to take over my thought processes. What was I going to do? After a few deep breaths, I decided the first thing to do was contact the dispatcher via radio so he could contact all the other folks that needed to know. I told him it would be necessary to hold all trains until I was released from the site. I then called Tower 19, which controlled trains from several railroads at an interlocker just a mile from my location, and advised the operator that it would be necessary to hold trains.

In just a few minutes my radio became very busy. The dispatcher was relaying questions from about a dozen different agencies. Then the tower operator called with more questions. Was the person still alive, male or female, nationality, exact location - dozens of questions and I didn't have that many answers. I finally decided I needed to try and get down to where the body was so that I could answer their questions. After all, I couldn't even say for certain if they were alive or dead.

I pulled ahead to the end of the bridge and began to climb down though the tangled driftwood. This was not one of my smartest decisions, but me and 'smart' don't always get along. After what seemed like hours of wandering though this maze of driftwood, I finally reached my desti-nation and after moving a few pieces of wood, I finally had a full view. There it was: one of J C Penney's finest mannequins.

Real dread replaced my state of panic as I climbed back to my vehicle, realizing that I probably had every train in the Dallas area stopped. If I thought there were a lot of questions before, you should have heard all that I heard after I got back on the radio and said, "Never mind."

I will say this: Despite the wishes of many, I didn't lose my job, but it took months for the story to die down. Even when relieving in East Texas and Louisiana I was sometimes known as "The Mannequin Man."

Oh well, this probably wouldn't be the worst thing to happen to me in the thirty-three years I had left to work on the railroad.

OLD JOHN

It was a particularly dark night as the mile long freight train made its way across the territory. The train had a full crew made up of an engineer, fireman and head brakeman on the locomotive, and a conductor and rear brakeman on the caboose. As the train would traverse around curves the crew would look back, or ahead if on the caboose, and inspect their train for possible problems such as sticking brakes, hot journals or hand brakes that had been overlooked before leaving the terminal.

As they looked back at their train, the crew on the locomotive saw sparks flying from one of the boxcars about halfway back. The engineer told them that he would ease the train up to where it was on a long straight portion of track and someone could walk back and check out the problem. As the train came to a stop, John, the head brakeman, stood up and said that he would walk back and take care of the problem, since it was probably just a handbrake that someone had left engaged.

John got off the engine with lantern in hand and started his walk back to the problem. The engineer watched John as he slowly walked away until finally all he could see was the glow of the lantern slowly swaying back and forth in the darkness. The engineer said, "Man, it's going to take old John forever to walk down there and climb that car, release the handbrake and get back up here to the head end. One of us should have gone."

Meanwhile, Old John had finally reached the boxcar that had a handbrake still set. The handbrake was up at the top of the car, and Old John would have to climb about ten feet up the side of the boxcar to release the brake. What John didn't realize was that the rear brakeman had already walked up the opposite side of the train and climbed up on the car and was ready to release the brake. John shined his lantern up to the brake and saw the rear brakeman. The rear brakeman did not have his lantern and asked John to pitch him his lantern so he could see how to release the brake. The rear brakeman caught the lantern, released the brake, tossed the lantern back to John and they both headed back to their assigned locations.

Meanwhile, back on the locomotive, the engineer, who had been watching the best that he could, said "I can't believe it!"

The fireman asked "What's going on?"

The engineer said "Old John just jumped from the ground up to the top of the car, released the hand brake, jumped back to the ground, and is heading back toward us!"

Old John had become a legend, at least until he got back on the locomotive.

DOG DAY

In the spring of 1976 I was sent to Kirbyville, Texas to relieve on a track supervisor position. A track supervisor patrols an assigned portion of track in a hy-rail pickup, inspecting the track, right-of-way, bridges, etc. and manages the work forces on that territory. This particular territory ran from Kirbyville, Texas, to Oakdale, Louisiana.

It was the second week of this particular assignment and I was beginning to feel comfortable with the territory and the people who were a part of it. I was hy-railing down the track on a beautiful, peaceful morning and as I came around a curve I slammed on the brakes and came to a quick stop. There in front of me was a dog in the middle of the track. Someone had chained the dog to each rail, and there was no way for it to clear the track.

Of course, the dog was frantic, having seen the headlights of my truck coming around the curve directly at him. I got out of the hy-rail truck and slowly approached the dog, speaking softly with my hand out in a friendly gesture. The dog continued to struggle, pulling at the chains, twisting and fighting to free himself. I stopped a few feet from him and squatted down, continuing to speak softly. After about ten minutes the dog began to settle down enough to where I could pet him. When I felt that he was calm enough I started to unchain him.

Suddenly he looked up over my shoulder and began to growl. I stood and turned just in time to see a rather large man walking from behind the pine trees directly toward me. He yelled something about what the hell was I doing with his dog. I told him it was none of his business unless he was the idiot that had tied the dog to the rail. He said something about he would take care of me, too, as he rapidly closed the distance between us.

I guess it was because he was in such a hurry to get in my face, but for some reason he had apparently not noticed the pick handle I was gripping in my right hand. Well, anyway, as I was helping him exit the railroad property, I felt certain that he understood my disdain for animal abuse and that if he was ever seen on railroad property again charges would be filed.

I finished unchaining the dog and we walked to the hy-rail truck. I opened the passenger door and he jumped in and sat in the front seat. As we hy-railed down the track, he just sat there looking over at me every once in a while as if wanting a little reassurance. He was just a plain old hound dog, but had a regal aura about him and deserved a loving companion. I had no idea what to do with him.

We hy-railed on to the next depot, where we stopped, shared my sandwich, and rested in the shade of the loading dock for awhile. The local train crew walked by and visited with us and played fetch with the dog. Before leaving the depot, I called the Hawkshaw (Santa Fe Police) and reported the incident, except I don't think I mentioned the pick handle. He said that he was pretty sure he knew the man, and that he would keep an eye on him for a while.

For the next two days the hound dog hy-railed the territory with me and stayed in my motel room at night. He was quite a companion. The next day was Friday and I was going home for the weekend, with no idea what I was going to do with the dog. We stopped at a depot to make a phone call or two. The local train crew had rolled into town right behind us. The conductor, a really good feller, walked up and started petting the dog and hem-hawing around until he finally asked what I was going to do with the dog. I told him I guessed that I would try to find someone to give him to before I left for home. A big smile came to his face and he said, "You found someone. I would be happy to take him and give him a good home!"

Come to find out, the old conductor had just lost his dog to age about a week before. It's sure nice when stories have happy endings.

DON'T CRY OVER SPILT WHISKEY

Years ago, in a small town on the Lampasas district in Texas, there was a Santa Fe agent who was known to take a sip or two of whiskey every once in a while. He was a good man who, for the most part, did his job in a manner that wouldn't attract much attention. He was sometimes forgetful and would doze off every once in a while. He had a young telegraph operator working with him, who would fill in the gaps and see that everything was taken care of by the end of each day.

One day an old farmer, a friend of the agent, stopped by the depot for a short visit. The agent said that he was out of whiskey and needed to figure out a way to replenish his supply. The farmer said that he was driving into Brownwood, and would be glad to go by the bootlegger's place and fetch him a bottle. However, it would be late before he returned because he had other business to tend to.

The agent called the young operator over and told him that he needed him to ride into Brownwood with the farmer and go by the bootlegger's and pick him up a bottle of whiskey. The farmer would then drop him off at the Brownwood depot and he could catch the 583 train that was scheduled to leave at 11:45 a.m. The operator pointed out that (a) the train was not scheduled to stop at their location and (b) there were rules against unauthorized persons riding on trains. The agent said he would give the train a stop signal on the semaphore signal at the depot; then he would be able to get off the train undetected.

The farmer and the operator headed for Brownwood. Once there, they stopped by the bootlegger's place and purchased the whiskey. Before leaving, the farmer called the bank to set a meeting time with them to take care of some financial business. He was told that the meeting was going to be rescheduled for another day. Upon hearing that news, the farmer told the operator that there was nothing else that he needed in Brownwood if he couldn't meet with the bank. He told the operator he would just drive him back to the depot. The operator was very happy that he was no longer going to stowaway on the train.

As they approached the depot, the operator noted that the agent, who didn't know he wasn't on the 583, had yet to give a stop indication on the depot semaphore signal and the 583 train would be by shortly. He told the farmer to let him out about a quarter of a mile from the depot. He then snuck down the opposite side of the track from the depot and hid in the weeds to see if the not-so-trusty agent would give the stop signal as planned. A short time later he could see headlight of the 583 train coming over the hill. There was still no stop signal.

The engines of the train blew by the depot at about 50 MPH with dust, loose papers, and grass rolling up along the side of the train as it passed. As he peered between the wheels of the train as it rolled by, he could see the agent running out of the depot and standing on the other side. The operator rubbed dirt and grass on his clothes and messed up his hair. As soon as the train had passed, he slowly stood up from the weeds and began dusting the dirt and grass from his clothes as he staggered up on the tracks.

The agent ran over to him and grabbed him by both arms and looked into his face with tears coming from his eyes and with a quiver in his voice said, "You didn't break the bottle, did you?"

DIRTY DOUGHERTY

Over the course of my railroading career, I worked thirteen different jobs as I climbed the corporate ladder and then climbed back down. The Santa Fe had some interesting and unique people take part in making it a proud and successful entity, and I have had the privilege of knowing many of them. They range from gandy dancers to Presidents.

One such person was Don Flick. Don worked for me as a gandy dancer (trackman) on several of my gangs in Texas and Oklahoma back in the mid 1970's. On the railroad, Don was known as Dirty Dougherty, as very few railroaders were called by their actual name. The Dougherty part was because he was from Dougherty, Oklahoma. The Dirty part, well, you only had to see him to understand that part. It wasn't that he had bad hygiene. He would arrive for work every morning clean and most presentable. But, after he had worked no longer than fifteen minutes or so, he would have become one with the dirt, grease and creosote associated with the work he was performing. He got close to his work.

Don was a heck of a man in his younger days. He stood six feet six inches tall, weighed 300+ pounds, and by his own admission had weighed as much as 450 pounds. He had bright red curly hair that came down to his shoulders. His beard was full and very red. He had full red eye brows to match, and there wasn't much space between the eye brows and his hairline.

I can recall the first time I worked with Don. He had already been given the Dirty Dougherty tag, but I didn't know how well he accepted that name, so I called him Don when addressing him directly. Then, after he had been with my gang for several days, it happened. We were having a particularly tough day, and I turned to Don and said, "Damn it, Dirty Dougherty, get over here and give us a hand." As soon as it came out of my mouth I realized this might not be good. There was silence for what seemed like an eternity as Don slowly turned and walked toward me.

I know you have seen those outdoor adventure movies when the star is approached by this huge Grizzly bear and as the Grizzly gets close he rares up on his back legs and looks like he is ten feet tall. That's the feeling I had. He walked up to me and gave me what I felt was a chilling glare. Then he said, "That would be Mr. Dirty Dougherty to you" and a big ol' smile came across his face. That was the day we became friends.

One evening I was home with the family in Cleburne, Texas, as I was fortunate to be working in the Cleburne area for a while. There was a heavy knock at the front door and before I could get out of my easy chair my three year old daughter, Shanon, ran over and opened the door. Her mouth fell open and the color left her face as she stepped back, pointed and said, "Sasquatch." I swooped her up in my arms and peered around the door. It was Dirty Dougherty.

He had dropped by to let me know that he wasn't going to be at work the next day on account of having to go home to Dougherty and take care of some family business. I invited him in for a glass of tea. That evening I saw another side of Don while he talked to and held my daughter as they laughed and he held Shanon's favorite doll. It was amazing to see this huge man sitting there talking in a childish manner and showing a softness that seemed perfectly natural to him.

In September 1976 my gang had moved to Wayne, Oklahoma where we were inserting a few new ties into the track. I had visions of moving up into a management position in the safety department and this was an important day in that quest. The head safety guy of Santa Fe and the assistant general manager of safety were going to come by and visit with my gang and me. I had informed those on the gang of the visit and asked them to work safely and do their jobs well. I wasn't concerned about anything and they shouldn't be either.

The dignitaries arrived shortly after lunch. We were walking through the worksite when the Director of Safety said to me, "Shouldn't you have two men carrying a tie?" I turned and there was Dirty Dougherty carrying a 200-lb. tie under one arm.

I hollered to him, "Say Don, let's double up on them ties!"

He responded, "I gotcha Boss. Sorry about that."

We continued our walk though the worksite and as we turned to walk back, there came Dirty Dougherty with a crosstie under each arm and a big ol' smile on his face. You gotta love him.

He's gone now. I miss Don Flick. May he rest in peace.

Day to Day, Year to Year, Boy to Man

PART IV

———————————◆———————————

Slowly he began to change, or maybe not so much change as return to the person he should have been. He had a family to be proud of: a wife who was beautiful, committed and very patient, as well as two beautiful daughters. He loved his family more than anything that had ever been a part of his being. He wanted them to have everything they needed. He wanted them to be happy and secure. In his mind, the way to provide all these things was with money. Money meant work, and work meant long hours, traveling all over the country and preparing for the next promotion with the good old Santa Fe.

At Christmas, the girls got gifts from Mom and Dad. Although Mom had done all the buying, wrapping, assembling and hiding, she always gave Dad credit. Dance recitals, gymnastics, twirling, and birthday parties were all taken care of by Mom, who always gave Dad as much credit as possible, and when it wasn't, she always explained how much Dad wanted to be there. The years seem to fly by and one day he sat down, took a deep breath, looked around and saw his beautiful daughters had become beautiful young ladies. He was proud, yet he was sad. They were leaving home and he needed more time. He would sit and slowly flip through photographs of the family and think, "I should have been there more."

Then his wife would sit beside him, put her hand on his leg, smile, and say, "We did good, Sweetie."

I AIN'T GUILTY, IT'S MY BROTHER

In 1978 I was promoted to a management position. After working for the railroad for seven years, I felt comfortable with my working knowledge of first line supervision, but knew I had a lot to learn in almost every aspect of management. I was really fortunate that I was surrounded by experienced people who came from every aspect of the railroad operation. I watched, listened to and tagged along with some of the most impressive management figures that I had ever been around, absorbing their philosophies and techniques and using them to form my own managerial style.

Just as I was beginning to feel comfortable with my progress, I was informed that I needed to educate myself and be prepared to be Chairman and officiate over formal investigations. On the railroad, a formal investigation is held when an employee is accused of a rules infraction that could result in discipline, suspension or dismissal. The procedure is similar to a trial without a jury. The Chairman is the Judge and the charged employee may ask for representation by a union official. As in a trial, the charges are read, witnesses are called, evidence is brought, arguments are made and then a decision is rendered.

I sat in as an observer on several formal investigations and had read through the transcripts of several more, when I received a call from the Superintendent who informed me that I was scheduled to hold a formal investigation the following week. I immediately went into a panic on the inside, while on the outside I assured the Superintendent that I would be ready. I began to gather all the information I would need for the investigation: a copy of the charges filed, a list of potential witnesses, the personnel records of the charged employee, as well as the witnesses and transcripts of several investigations that the probable union representative had participated in, so I would know what to expect from him. I locked myself in my office for several days studying and preparing for the big event. I took it all home with me and worked until the early morning hours for several days. I wrote notes on every possible action and reaction that I could think of. As the scheduled day approached I felt ready. Nervous and tired, but ready. I had not studied that hard since school. Come to think of it, I never really studied that hard *in* school.

The day arrived. I was pumped as I sat in my office going over hundreds of note cards. About thirty minutes before the investigation was scheduled, there was a knock on my office door. It was the charged employee. He asked if he could speak to me for a minute. I asked if he needed his union representative present and he replied that he didn't. He sat down and then told me he thought we had him mixed up with his brother, who also worked for the railroad. He said it was his brother who had been stealing company material and selling it, and that he would never do anything like that. I told him we were not charging him with stealing company material. We were charging him with stealing time by claiming pay for time that he had not actually worked. He looked relieved, and asked what the discipline would be. I told him and he waived his right to have a formal investigation and agreed to the terms of the discipline.

I was glad that it was over, but was a little disappointed that I hadn't had a chance to show my stuff. However, all that studying and preparation I had done came in handy when I held the formal investigation on the brother who had stolen all the company material and then sold it for profit. You'll never guess who the star witness was.

For brothers, they really weren't that close.

IT'S NOT WHAT YOU THINK

For thirty-eight years I was "on call" seven days a week, twenty-four hours a day on the Santa Fe, and later, Burlington Northern Santa Fe Railroad. The money could be pretty good but there were times when I would have gladly exchanged the money for a little more "home time." I missed a lot of things that I now regret.

I recall one cold winter night, having been away nearly a week, that I decided to call home. My youngest daughter, probably two or three years old at the time, answered the phone. I said, "Hello kiddo, this is Daddy."

She said, "Daddy doesn't live here anymore." It broke my heart, and if I could have, I would have driven home that night. I missed my wife and two girls for so much of my railroad career.

Even when I was home, there were times that I would get called out several times during the night and end up sleeping through most of the day; then get up and go back to work. The winter months were usually the worst as far as getting called out to work. In cold weather, the rail portion of the tracks had a tendency to break or pull apart at the joints.

In cold weather the rail shrinks and becomes more brittle, and if there is a small defect in the rail, it can break. Another problem in cold weather is the rail joints. A joint is where two rails are connected with two heavy bars, with about six large bolts placed through the bars and the rails to hold the joint together. In cold weather these joints will pull apart, shearing the bolts off and leaving a gap between the two rails. This gap could be two to six inches and presented a hazard to passing trains. The railroad slang for this type of defect is "stripped joint."

One winter night the temperature dropped into the teens, and sure enough the phone rang. It was the dispatcher, who stated that there was a suspected rail problem and that my services were needed. My wife and kids were still up and I told my wife that I had to go to work. I got dressed and kissed the girls goodbye. My wife asked where I was going and how long did I think I would be. I told her that it was probably a "stripped joint" and that I should be back in a couple of hours.

About an hour after I left, my mother-in-law (Nanny) called the house and my four year old daughter answered the phone. Nanny asked if she could speak to Mama. My daughter told her that her Mama was in the bedroom, so Nanny asked her where her Daddy was. My sweet little girl said "Daddy has gone to a strip joint, and he said he would be back in a couple of hours."

My wife says that she was able to explain the situation to her mother, but I'm not sure Nanny ever looked at me the same again.

WATER UNDER THE BRIDGE

———————

Years ago, out in the piney woods of East Texas, there was an old depot agent who was as fine a fellow as you would ever want to be around. He was friendly, hard working, and had a heart as big as life itself. He did, however, have one fault. He was a talker. Once you engaged him in conversation, you were lucky if you could disengage him. If you asked him a simple question, you always got a lot more than you had asked for. Talking to him was like getting a drink out of a fire hydrant: You always got more than you wanted.

Most people understood him and accepted him as he was, a devoted and lovable man. However, his talkativeness also ran over into his correspondence at work. His business letters rambled on and on. Back at this time, the agents would send wires to other agencies on the railroad such as the superintendent's office, the trainmaster's office and many others. It would cost the company a fee, based on how many words or spaces were used in each wire.

This cost came to the attention of the superintendent's office and the agent was confronted and instructed to immediately change his wordy habits when it came to sending wires. He was to only include pertinent information and keep the verbiage down to an absolute minimum. The agent found this very difficult and he received several more visits concerning his wordiness, with each visit being a little more harsh, until he was finally told that his time for changing was running out.

Spring arrived, and with it came heavy rains. It rained for days, and flooding began to be a problem on the railroad. Portions of track and bridges were beginning to wash out. In this particular part of East Texas, there was a long bridge over a creek that had a history of washing out. A problem developed, since with all the roads closing and the associated water problems, no one could reach the bridge to inspect it. It would be necessary to know the bridge's status in order to form an operating plan for running trains.

Finally the superintendent called the agent, knowing he lived near the bridge, and asked him if he would inspect the bridge and then send a wire to all involved as to the bridge's status. Everyone was waiting anxiously for his information in order to come up with a plan.

Finally the wire from the old agent came. The message was brief: "The water is where the bridge was!"

I guess they finally got their point across to the talkative old agent.

THE ATCHISON TOPEKA & TOM
CRUISE RAILROAD

One thing you never wanted the railroad to know was that you liked your present work location or headquarters. It seemed that the more you liked a location, the shorter the time before you were transferred. I loved working and living in the Temple area, and couldn't have asked for a greater crowd of friends to work with. I managed to keep it all a secret for ten years. Then, in 1988, somebody found out about my fond feelings for the area, the people and the fact that I had two young children in school, so they transferred me to Fort Worth. They apparently did not do their homework, or they would have found that I worked in the Fort Worth/Dallas area before moving to Temple, and was very fond of that area as well.

The new headquarters office was to be in Euless, Texas. However, until the new building was made railroad ready, my office and the Texas Region Headquarters would temporarily be housed in the old Division Headquarters building in downtown Fort Worth next door to the Santa Fe depot. We had barely settled into our new surroundings and routines when the regional manager called me into his office and informed me of a "little" project he wanted me to help take care of.

The project involved making myself available to and assisting a movie production company that was going to use the Fort Worth Santa Fe depot and the adjacent tracks in the making of a movie. I was also to protect the company's interest and coordinate, as much as practical, their needs. The director of this movie was a fellow by the name of Oliver Stone and one of the actors was Tom Cruise. I believe the movie was something called "Born on the Fourth of July."

On the day of their arrival, it was hard to believe the number of trucks, trailers, campers, people and just stuff in general that the production company brought in. We met with some of the production people to discuss their needs. Oliver Stone didn't make the meeting, but I believe I met him the next day when he asked me where the men's room was.

They explained that the Santa Fe depot was perfect in almost every detail for what they wanted, except it needed to be Penn Central Station. They talked of needing to move existing furniture and bring in more to add to it. They would need to change the lighting with lights, mirrors and drapes. They would need to hide the hundreds of Santa Fe logos throughout the depot and on adjacent buildings. All automobiles would have to be moved and the railroad would have to be shut down for an hour or so. They indicated that some walls would have to be painted and some temporary walls built. I was thinking that this was going to take a week or so to complete but when asked how long all this would take, one of the production guys said it might take as long as half a day. He went on to say that after the shoot was completed everything would be returned to its original appearance.

It was amazing to see them work. It was like a swarm of bees or an army of ants had enveloped the area. During this process I met Tom Cruise's assistant. She had approached me about some of the particular needs of her boss. I was able to accommodate her, and in appreciation she said that she could introduce me to Tom Cruise if things worked out right. Even though I hadn't asked for the introduction and I really wasn't a fan, I got to thinking it would be nice, especially to tell my wife and kids who *were* fans.

In practically no time, the transformation was completed. It was unbelievable how, in so short a time, the entire area had been transformed into a completely different time and location. I was helping set up the locomotive and passenger cars that were to be used in the filming when I looked over and saw Tom Cruise and his assistant standing near the rear of the depot. The assistant motioned to me and walked toward me. I would like to say this was the beginning of a long lasting and close personal relationship between me and Tom, but it didn't happen.

The assistant advised me that Mr. Cruise was late for a series of meetings and that an introduction wouldn't be possible. Even though she too was busy, she took time to express their appreciation for all of our help and introduced me to several other interesting people in connection with the movie. It was clear to me that what was fun and very exciting for me was an everyday occurrence for them.

Everything seemed to go well. It seemed to me that there was an awful lot of time, money and work that went into about an hour of filming. It was amazing how fast things where returned to normal. Within just a few hours things were again transformed from a Hollywood set to an old Santa Fe depot. There wasn't a hint that they were ever there.

Sadly, I never found time to go see the movie.

MARK

Mark was one of about twenty men who were hired in one group by the Santa Fe Railroad back in the early to mid 1970's. It was unusual for that many new hires to come from one particular area, especially an area in Oklahoma that the railroad didn't even run through. However, they were all young, strong and for the most part didn't mind a little hard work.

I had just been assigned to the foreman's position on a brand new gang with a brand new quarter-million dollar machine and four new-hire trackmen, of which Mark was one. He was about 6'2" and weighed about 200 lbs. with light blond hair. In the beginning he didn't have much to say, but showed a natural ability and willingness to learn.

On the third day of the gang's existence, we were told by the train dispatcher that it would be several hours before we could get our machine out on the main track to work. I told the machine operator to stay with his machine and I took the four trackmen with me to the worksite to do a little hand work and prep the site for when we could bring the machine out. I had told the dispatcher my plan and he told me that there was a northbound train coming, but that it was going to stop and do some work in Saginaw so I would have forty-five minutes before the train went through my work area. One of the things we needed to do was remove some road crossing planks from a private road crossing so that the machine could do its work though that area.

Each wooden plank was about eight feet long, three feet wide, about six inches thick and weighed several hundred pounds. Each plank was held in place by huge screws that were about a foot long and went through the plank into the crossties in the track. The crossing screws had been damaged, so we weren't able to remove them with the normal tool. I decided that we had time to place large track jacks under one end of the plank and jack the boards upward until the screws pulled up out of the ties.

We had one end of the plank jacked up to where it was about a foot above the rail, but the screws in the other end of the plank were still holding firmly. Then I heard something that sent chills running down my spine. It was a train whistle. Apparently the train was coming well ahead of what the dispatcher had figured. I told the men to remove the jacks from under the plank. With the jacks removed, the plank remained about a foot above the rail. I looked back over my shoulder and I could see the headlight of the train about a half mile away. Even if I tried to flag the train, it would not have time to stop. I looked up at the faces of the men. They had no idea what was happening. I knew I needed to get the plank back down because I felt certain it would derail the train, but I also knew that these new men would be of no help and it would be better to get them out of harm's way. I hollered for them to move all the tools from the track and to get on the other side of the right-of-way fence.

With the men in the clear, I grabbed a sixteen pound sledge hammer and began beating down on the plank with all my might. I could hear the train whistle blowing closer and closer, and could hear my men yelling that the train was getting close. I realized that the sledge hammer wasn't doing the job so I threw it aside and grabbed a track jack, that weighed about sixty pounds, and began slamming it down on the plank. It began going down, but not fast enough. I turned toward the train, which was now only a quarter of a mile away and whistling furiously. I was about to abandon my efforts when I heard a thud behind me. It was Mark. He had grabbed another track jack and was beating down on the plank. I joined him and together we struck the plank about a half dozen more times. I threw my jack one direction, and Mark threw his the other as we cleared the track. The train rumbled past with its whistle blowing continuously and dust and loose grass rolling along beside the train. The cowcatcher on the lead locomotive cleared the plank about two inches.

It became clear to me that day that Mark was a hell of a man, and a good person to have your back. On the job, Mark became my go-to guy. If there was a job to do, no matter how difficult the challenge, he never waited to be told. He would just get the job done. Off the job, Mark and I became friends, and because we were both single, did our share of running around. As the gang moved from town to town and state to state, Mark stayed on my gang. It seemed that in our after-work ventures he always kind of took care of me when we were in Oklahoma, and I took care of him in Texas. I was dating my future wife (Amber) and when we were working in the DFW area the three of us would go out and have a good time. Mark could be a real respectful gentleman when necessary, just as he could be a real hell raiser when it wasn't. Amber liked him and seemed to be less worried about some of my out-of-town shenanigans if he was with me.

We became as brothers and shared openly most things on our mind. He told me about his mom and dad being divorced. He told me that his dad never got over the divorce and had committed suicide. He told me he was divorced himself, but still loved his ex-wife deeply. And, there was a time or two he talked about his concern that he was following the same trail that his dad had gone down. I would assure him that he was nothing like his dad in that respect. I would remind him that he had too many things going for him to be thinking like that. It was hard for me to believe he could even think about his life that way.

Time went on, and so did our friendship. There was a lot of partying, a lot of hard work and a continued closeness and respect. Amber and I got married, and I was promoted to a track supervisor's position. Mark bumped around from gang to gang and as his seniority would allow, he would try to work back in Oklahoma, closer to home. We would run across each other every once in a while and catch up on each other's life, but the reunions became fewer as time passed. Then I was promoted into management, and was being moved to a different division of the railroad. Before I left, I contacted Mark and told him that I was leaving, and also told him that I could get him promoted to a foreman's job before I left. He thanked me, but said he really preferred working as a trackman and would rather not have the responsibility of a foreman. I told him to let me know if he ever changed his mind, and told him I would stay in touch.

My family and I moved to Temple, and I began my career in railroad management. Things were hectic for a while - new home, new job, new people. I spent more time than I realized getting settled at home and at work. From time to time I would call around and try to track down Mark, as well as other friends back in the home division, but never had much luck, other than they thought Mark had been working up in Oklahoma for a long while. Then one day I happened to run into an old foreman buddy of mine from back home. I asked him if he had any idea where that blond haired Okie Mark was. He paused, and then told me that Mark was dead. I could feel the blood rush to my face, and although I was afraid to ask, I turned back to him and asked what had happened. Knowing that Mark and I had been close, he paused again, and I knew. Mark had committed suicide.

I walked back to my office and slammed the door in anger. I threw things from one side of the room to the other. I cursed him for not believing in the things I had shared with him. I was so angry that he was gone, and I didn't even know it. He had cheated so many people out of all the things that he had to offer. He was gone, and he didn't have to be. I sat back in my chair and I could see his smiling face. I could still feel the touch of his firm handshake the last time I saw him and we said goodbye. I leaned back, took a deep breath and I cried.

WE'RE RAILROADING NOW

O ut of all the positions I worked with the Santa Fe, and later the Burlington Northern Santa Fe, the trainmaster position was probably one of the most challenging as well as most interesting. As trainmaster I had responsibility over the Greater Fort Worth Terminal area which also included Cleburne, Saginaw and parts of the Dallas area. Almost every day there would be several interesting happenings, some of which would be good, some bad and some just plain scary.

My responsibilities would range from trivial one minute to life threatening the next. One morning, about 2:00 a.m., while sleeping soundly in the old home bed, I received a phone call from a distraught switch crew at Saginaw who said they had been sitting on their engine for over an hour, waiting for a limo to take them to the yard office to eat, but that the assistant trainmaster had yet to send one. I asked how far they were from the yard office, and they replied that they were at least a quarter of a mile or maybe even further away. As I recall I paused (I may have counted to ten) and then told them to climb their butts down from the engine and walk to the yard office. I warned them that if they ever called me at 2:00 a.m. for anything such as this again, I would be happy to get up, get dressed and drive the twenty-five miles and make the rest of their shift miserable.

I can also recall a cool Fall day at the Saginaw yard when I heard a northbound train call the assistant trainmaster on the radio and informed him that he was approaching from the south and would be heading into the yard in order to set out some cars before continuing on north to Gainesville, Texas. I decided to drive down to the south end of the yard and observe the train as it entered the yard. While setting next to the south switching lead, I saw a consist of about five or six Union Pacific locomotives coming out of a track and heading south. I looked to the south and could see the headlight of the northbound train about to enter the yard. I grabbed my radio and called the UP crew, who had brought an interchange delivery of about one hundred cars about forty-five minutes earlier, and told them to stop their locomotives. I received no response, so I jumped out of my vehicle and began to give hand signals for the consist to stop. The locomotives still did not stop and as they moved closer, I could finally see that there was not anyone on them. I called the approaching northbound train on the radio and advised them to stop their train and be prepared to abandon their locomotive. I was then able to mount the moving locomotives as they passed my location and stop them. I then backed them into the clear, lined all the switches properly and allowed the northbound train to continue into the yard.

Needless to say, things could have been a lot worse and the Union Pacific crew, normally a very good crew, received the appropriate attention for their failure to set any brakes and secure the consist before going to lunch. One thing for sure: I had that particular UP crew in my pocket for a long time. They, too, knew it could have been much worse, and were more than happy to help me out any way they could.

Then there was the day that a switch crew thought they were rolling four loaded liquid petroleum tank cars into a track that already had cars in it, tied down, with brakes set. They uncoupled the cars and were allowing them to slowly roll to what they thought would be a soft coupling with the cars in the track. The problem was, someone had lined the wrong switch and the cars entered a clear track. The switching yard is downhill southbound and the cars continued to roll through the track picking up speed as they rolled. The cars rolled all the way to the south end of the yard and derailed, overturning onto their sides and sliding all the way off the right-of-way and across Fort Worth's Main Street, directly across from Meacham Airport and completely blocking the road.

The Fort Worth police arrived quickly and began to protect the derailment site. Some of the police officers began to cover a two or three mile radius warning people there could be no smoking, no welding, no open flames of any kind. Shortly after I arrived at the scene, the head mechanical officer also arrived and ran over to me, saying that we needed to clear the area until it could be determined if any of the four liquid petroleum cars were leaking. I told him that, in my opinion, I didn't think there was a gas leak. He asked how I knew there was no leakage. I pointed over to the cars lying in the street, and told him that while the police were covering the area warning people about open flames, welding and smoking, the officers who stayed at the scene had lit flares and placed them next to the LPG cars to keep people from running into them. I'd never seen eyes almost pop out of someone's head until that moment.

Obviously, it was a very lucky day.

Day to Day, Year to Year, Boy to Man

PART V

———————◆———————

Things began to change. Things had probably been changing for a while, but he had been too busy to notice. The changes had happened in all aspects of his life. His girls had grown up. The railroad that had consumed so much of his time and efforts was, in his mind, changing into something less than the great organization that he had served for so many years. Stress began to creep into his already hectic work schedule, and the job that he had always given himself to unconditionally had turned into a thing of dread.

He turned to the one constant in his life, and with his head bowed into his hands, he released all that was weighing on him to his loving wife. He was somewhat ashamed of what he had to say, but knew it was time. He told her that his heart was no longer into the management positions he had worked so hard to obtain on the railroad. And he explained that, even though there were still potential promotional moves, he had lost the energy and drive it would take to advance. She squeezed his hand, reminding him that she had told him years before that she would support whatever job decisions he made concerning his beloved railroad as long as the family went where he went. The next morning he asked for and was granted a meeting with his superintendent. He advised the superintendent that effective as soon as possible, he was going to give up his management position, exercise his seniority, and finish his career as a scheduled employee. He walked out of that office almost twenty seven years from the date he went to work for the railroad, and almost twenty years after entering management.

He felt like the weight of the world had been lifted from his shoulders.

RAILROADIN'—THEN AND NOW

In 1973 I was working on my third year with the Santa Fe Railroad and my first few months as an Extra gang foreman. I had not completely convinced myself that I wanted to railroad for the rest of my life, but the money was pretty good and I had managed to get promoted three times in less than two years. Looking back, I would like to say that I was ambitious, but I may have been a little overbearing or cocky at times. I was always fair with those who worked for me, but I was highly competitive when it came to promotions and with those who sought those same promotions.

I had a gang working between Brownwood and Fort Worth. The gang was composed of ten men, a couple of on-track machines and a large gang truck. One Friday morning, the roadmaster met with me, and informed me of a specific job he would like for us to accomplish before we quit for the weekend. He warned me that it might be difficult to accomplish because it looked like there was going to be a lot of train traffic, and the train dispatcher might not allow us to occupy the track with our machines. Also, because of recent heavy rains, we wouldn't be able to drive to the work location via the right-of-way road. The roadmaster was anxious to repair the track at this location because there was a slow order over that portion of the track, slowing trains down to ten miles per hour. I assured him we would do everything we could to get the track repaired and the slow order removed.

I spoke with the train dispatcher about the work location, and told him I would need at least two hours to occupy the track with my machines in order to make the repairs. As expected, he informed me that train traffic was too heavy for him to allow the machines on the track. I told the men to load up in the truck and follow me so we would see how close we could drive to the work location. We arrived at a location where the road crossed the tracks about one and a half miles from where we needed to work. As expected, the right-of-way road was muddy with standing water. There was no way that the large gang truck would be able to traverse the road without becoming stuck in the mud. The work location was too far to walk and carry the heavy tools we would need to make repairs. It was beginning to look as if the work was going to have to wait for another day.

After sitting and thinking for a while, I called the men together and told them I had a plan I would like to try. If it worked out, we would call it quits and go home early for the weekend. "Early quits", especially on Friday, was always a popular incentive for the men, so without even hearing my plan they agreed. I instructed them to get the tools that we would need for the job and to put them in the back of my personal pickup. I had a 1972 Chevy Luv pickup. It was Chevrolet's version of the Datsun (later to become Nissan) compact pickup.

I then selected four of the biggest and strongest men to go with me. At 6'1", and weighing about 220 lbs., I was the runt of the group. One of the men rode up front with me, and the others got in the bed of my truck. With everyone secure, we began our one and a half mile trip down the boggy road beside the track. Mud was flying everywhere as we went slip sliding on our way. Eventually we would bog down and become stuck in our tracks. We would all get out and gather around the rear of the pickup and pick it up and set it over enough to get out of the ruts we had made. Then we would walk around to the front and do the same there. Then we were off again, slinging mud as we went. We had to repeat our little set-over maneuver about four or five times before we finally reached the work location.

The work site was on straight track, with visibility of about one mile in each direction and with trains having to slow down to ten miles per hour, because of the slow order covering the location, I knew that we would either be able to clear the track in time for the train to pass or, if necessary, stop the train until we could clear the track. We went on about our work. After an hour and a half, even with letting a couple of trains get past us, we finished the job. We loaded ourselves and our equipment into the little Chevy Luv, and began slip sliding our way back to the main road, bogging down again four or five times and each time getting out and performing our set-over maneuver.

We arrived back with the rest of the gang, and transferred the tools back into the gang truck. After telling them how much I appreciated their help, I told the men to head back to headquarters, secure the truck and equipment, and head home. I stopped by a car wash and cleaned the mud from my once white pickup, then headed for the depot to take care of my paperwork. I called the dispatcher and told him to void the ten mile per hour slow order, because the track had been repaired. He was shocked and said that he never knew we were out among all the trains. I then called the roadmaster and informed him that we had taken care of the work he wanted done, and voided the slow order on the track. He was very pleased and asked how in the world we had accomplished the work with the heavy train traffic and muddy conditions. After hearing it might be best if he didn't know, he told me to tell the men they did a good job, and let them go early for the weekend. I told him we appreciated it and that I would let them know about the early quit.

Flash forward to 2007, not long before I retired. I had a gang working on my territory with a young foreman. I asked him to work a location on the track and then gave him several secondary locations to work. He and the gang arrived at the work site at approximately 8:30 a.m., called the train dispatcher and asked for authority to work at that location. The dispatcher told him that he had too many trains, and they would have to wait to do the work. The foreman and his gang sat there until 3:00 p.m. and without doing any work all day, went back to their tie up point and quit for the day. I did have a discussion with the foreman, but to maintain the PG rating of this writing, have chosen to omit the conclusion of this portion of the story.

There have been a lot of changes on the railroad over the years, some for the better, some not. It is for this reason that I share some of my history and the history that was passed to me by good men and women who came from a great railroad tradition. It is my hope that through my ramblings and the stories of other old-head railroaders, people will understand what is really meant when we say, "That's when railroaders were really railroadin'."

EVERYTHING, EVEN THE KITCHEN SINK

Between June 25, 1971 and August 15, 2007, I worked as a gandy dancer, machine operator, student foreman, foreman, track supervisor (track inspector), safety supervisor, brakeman, conductor, engineer, manager of safety and rules, trainmaster and assistant superintendent. While working almost all these jobs, at one time or another, I was either finding things on or near the railroad tracks that didn't belong there, or was charged with the investigation of such findings.

Those items included trash cans, doghouses, outhouses, automobiles (both junkers and those less than a day old), bicycles, tricycles, motorcycles, every toy known to man or child, septic tanks, tires, trees, fifty-five gallon barrels of oil, couches, chairs, beds, rocks, crossties, lumber, a half-naked woman, bathtubs, commodes, hobos, guns, a couple hein' and shein' in the back of a pickup, cattle, pets of every kind, trailers, machinery, traffic signs and cones, suitcases, three bedroom house, swing set, and lawn furniture. The list could go on forever.

Some of these things were found prior to being hit by a train, and some were reported after being struck. There is a story connected with almost every item listed. As you would think, the three bedroom house found on the tracks is an interesting tale. This house was found sitting on the track by an eastbound freight train moving about forty-five miles per hour. No, the train was not able to get stopped.

This old farm house had been sitting less than a quarter of a mile from the tracks for over fifty years. As viewed from an eastbound train, the house had always appeared to be sitting on the tracks until the train was about two tenths of a mile away, then you could see that the track curved to the left and never got any closer than a quarter of a mile to the house. The engineer stated that on that particular day, as he approached that location, the house appeared to be sitting in the same location it had been in for the ten years that he had been running on that territory.

What the engineer did not know was that on that particular day, the new owner of the house was having the house moved from its present location to a location about one mile the other side of the tracks. The house owner, or his movers, had failed to notify the Santa Fe railroad of the move as required by law. As they attempted to traverse the road crossing at this location, they had managed to become lodged against the rail and couldn't move forward or backward.

The engineer 'big holed', a term meaning that he placed the train in emergency braking, about two tenths of mile from the house and after his three locomotives and about twenty-five of his rail cars had passed through the house, the train stopped. Fortunately, there were no injuries other than some hurt feelings.

An investigation of the site revealed that what had once been a three bedroom house was now a one and one half bedroom house with a nice large breezeway. After the train had been moved, a walking inspection was made of the track. As we walked about a thousand feet past where the house had been struck, resting there in the middle of the track was the kitchen sink.

From that day on I could truthfully say that I had indeed found it all lying out on the railroad tracks, even the kitchen sink.

LIKE IT NEVER HAPPENED

If you were a railroader for any length of time, you heard hundreds of stories. Most were colorful recollections of past events, sometimes so farfetched they would be hard to believe, especially for non-railroaders. The stories were always exciting, many times humorous, and occasionally true.

One such story involves a particular train crew back in the day when the average length of a train was about a mile. Every train had a caboose, with the crews being made up of an engineer, head brakeman and sometimes a fireman on the locomotives and a conductor and rear brakeman on the caboose. Everyone on the crew had responsibilities during a trip. While the engineer and the conductor both had the bulk of the responsibilities, it was the conductor who was charged with the responsibility of getting all the work done en route in a proper manner, as well as taking care of most of the paperwork.

If conductors had been ranked as to their abilities, personality and work ethics, this particular conductor would be ranked at the very bottom. He was know by all to be lazy, hard to get along with and may have dabbled in the consumption of alcoholic beverages before, during and after going on duty. It was not unusual for this conductor to sack out on one of the caboose bunks and sleep though the entire trip and any of the work done en route.

Even though most of the crews were aware of this conductor's problems, it was not the common practice at that time to turn in or report fellow employees. However it was not uncommon for crews to handle these type situations themselves without involving management. The day had come for this crew to take action. The crew all met at the yard office at their on-duty point. As usual, the conductor was late arriving. The engineer and the two brakemen conceived a plan that was to take place on this trip that would hopefully serve as a wakeup call for the wayward conductor.

The conductor finally arrived, the crew boarded their train and while the rest of the crew were performing their required duties in preparation for departure, the conductor made himself comfortable on the caboose bunk. Shortly, the crew departed the terminal on their six thousand feet of train. As expected, the conductor was asleep and snoring within a few minutes of departure. After assuring the unconscious state of his conductor, the rear brakeman went to the rear of the caboose and removed the face of the air gauge. A train's braking power is provided by air. There has to be a certain amount of air pressure maintained throughout the train for the brakes to properly function. This gauge is there to provide the crew on the caboose with the ability to determine that there is adequate air pressure all the way to the rear of the train. After removing the air gauge face, the rear brakeman forced the indicator arrow down to zero and secured it there with a piece of gum.

This would cause an unsuspecting person to think that there was no air pressure to the caboose, thus there was no means of applying the brakes on the rear of the train. After completing his task, the rear brakeman picked up the train radio handset and clicked the transmission button three times. This was the predetermined signal to the engineer that the gauge had been disabled and the conductor was asleep. By this time the train was moving about fifty-five miles per hour.

Upon hearing the signal from the caboose, the engineer picked up the radio handset and began to transmit, "Emergency, emergency, emergency! Our train has come uncoupled and pulled apart about halfway back in the train! I will let you know when we have come to a stop on the head end of the train!"

Hearing this transmission on the loud speaker on the caboose, the conductor sat up quickly on the bunk, turned to the side window and peered out at the telegraph poles flying by. He then jumped up, staggered back to the rear of the caboose and looked up at the air gauge showing zero air pressure.

About that time, the engineer again came on the radio and stated, "The head end of the train is coming to a stop right..........NOW!"

The conductor, the color now gone from his face, again looked out the window at the telegraph poles flying by at fifty-five miles per hour, looked up at the air gauge one more time, and with a pathetic groan of profanity and his eyes rolling upward, fell to the caboose floor like a limp dish rag.

After assuring that the conductor was still breathing and had only passed out, the rear brakeman dragged him back to the bunk and made him comfortable. He then went back to the air gauge and restored it to normal operation and climbed up into the cupola as if nothing had happened. Within a few minutes the old conductor sat up, looked out the window at the passing scenery then walked back to the rear of the caboose. After checking the air gauge, the conductor looked up at the brakeman and said with a shaky voice, "What's going on?"

The rear brakeman responded in a calm relaxed tone, "Not much, what's going on with you?"

The conductor waddled back to his desk and sat down. There was nothing said the rest of the trip. It appeared that the plan had worked. No one ever had a problem with that particular conductor again—he retired.

HAWKSHAW

I was sitting in my old leather easy chair the other night, trying to decide whether to go ahead and fall asleep or continue to battle my heavy eyes and finish the movie, when the house phone rang. I started not to answer it because anybody I know, or at least the ones I talk to on a regular basis, call me on my cell. After several rings, I reluctantly answered the phone. The person on the phone said, "Mr. Beck, there has been a major derailment down here in Somerville and we need you here as soon as possible." My heart was moved; my mind was flooded with memories and a smile grew from the depths of my soul. Then there was a laugh and he said, "I bet you don't have any idea who this is."

There was a rush of emotions as I said, "Yes, Howard, how could I not recognize Santa Fe's legendary Hawkshaw." There was a pause, and then Howard said he was tickled that I remembered him after all these years. He went on, saying he had kept up with my career for about twenty years but had noticed I had kind of disappeared over the last three years. He decided to track me down. I told him I was really glad he found me, and we began a conversation that lasted for over an hour.

I need to share some thoughts and meaningful information with you concerning Howard, so that you can better understand why I consider this man a true reflection of the character that was the mainstay of the Santa Fe. First, physically, it would help if you could visualize John Wayne. I remember Howard as being over six feet tall, weighing 250 pounds and being solid muscle. He always wore jeans, a belt with a big western belt buckle, western type shirts, cowboy boots and hat. When he was outside, he would almost always have a chew of tobacco in his mouth, and he was outside most of the time. He was an intimidating man even though he smiled most of the time.

Howard was a simple-worded man. He never wasted words, and could say more in fewer words than anyone I have ever been around. He was always painfully honest, and as a special agent for the Santa Fe police, he expected the same from everyone else, no matter what your title. Although a railroad special agent, he always claimed to be just an old railroad "hawkshaw", a longtime slang name for railroad police. He knew most everybody in that part of the country, and most everybody knew him. I remember several big derailments out in the country when land owners would not give superintendents or even general managers permission to cross their property for fear of damaging their land. Yet Howard could speak to them, giving his word that everything would be returned to its original state or better, even if he had to do it himself, and based on his word, they would allow us to cross their property with our equipment to get to our derailment site.

One day I was in the Somerville area and stopped by to visit with Howard. He received a call that a crew on a train coming into town had reported seeing three men enter a boxcar in their train. These men were escapees from jail, and considered dangerous. Howard called the crew and told them to stop their train near the depot. Howard walked down to the boxcar in question, grabbed hold of the door latch, and slid the door all the way open with one quick move. You need to understand that normally it takes several people, or even a tractor, to open most boxcar doors. Howard looked into the car, raised his huge hand, pointed at the men and said, "You fellers come on down from there and don't make me hurt you." The men never said a word. They jumped down from the car and lay face down on the ground just as Howard had instructed them to do. Although Howard had a pistol on his hip, he never removed it from its holster. The sheriff's department quickly arrived and took the men in custody. Howard walked back to where I was standing and said, "After we get off work, you want to come out to the house and do some fishin'?"

Howard worked long hours on the railroad. After work, he would go home to his place and take care of his livestock, and then, if there was any rodeo-ing going on, he would be right in the middle of it. Although he didn't care about fishing himself, he loved to have folks out to fish in his stock ponds. I traveled a lot with our superintendent and asked Howard if I could bring him by sometime and do a little fishing, being that he loved to fish. Howard said "Shore 'nuff, anytime." After that, anytime we were in the area we would holler at Howard and stop by for a little fishing. Out there on that tank dam we were just buddies with no titles. Howard would never fish but would delight in seeing us fish and enjoying the visitation.

Howard epitomized the things that I love and remember about the "old" railroad. People like him are what gave the railroad its mystique and character. I'm not sure that folks like Howard ever received the recognition they deserved for making the Santa Fe railroad the majestic leader of its industry. I have often thought of Howard and others like him. I am ashamed that it had been over twenty years since we visited.

I am so glad I answered the phone. We relived so many good times. We shared the solemn respect felt for those friends and coworkers who had passed. He asked when I was going to come down for a little fishing, and then said, "Shoot, we don't even have to fish - we could just sit on the porch and visit for a while." As we were winding down our talk, he said that he had a lot of railroad stuff that he had collected over the years and he just wondered if I might want them. He said he wanted them to go to someone who would appreciate what they stood for. He then said he and cancer had been having one "hell of a battle" and that he wasn't sure how much time he had left.

Before I could respond he said, "Well, I got to go to bed. Got to get up early and feed the cows."

ME, THE RAILROAD AND BOB

It was a dark foggy night in Fort Worth, Texas. As was the case on too many of my nights, I had been called out by the train dispatcher due to a track indication. A track indication is when the dispatcher's board shows there is something occupying a track circuit when he does not show that anything should be there. I arrived at the location, called the train dispatcher, received authority to occupy the track and placed my hy-rail vehicle on the track and began my inspection.

After traveling only a short distance on the rail, I observed something lying across the rails. I stopped, grabbed my spotlight and spike maul handle, which I kept behind the seat to always carry when out at night, and began to walk down the track. Someone had laid a metal bar across the rails which would shunt or short out the circuit, causing the dispatcher's board to show that portion of track to be occupied.

As I reached down to remove the piece of metal from the track, I heard something move behind me. I gripped the maul handle and wheeled around with my heart in my throat. There stood a huge man in a tattered jacket, with a full beard and an old Texas Rangers ball cap on his matted hair. He raised his hands, as if to say he didn't want to be introduced to my spike maul handle, and smiled. As my spotlight finally settled on his face, I recognized him. Although I had never spoken to him, I saw him either walking or sitting along the right of way almost every day as I hy-railed through this part of my territory. As I passed him, he would always take off his cap and wave.

"What are you up to, being out this late at night, Bro?" I asked. He removed his cap, stammered for a moment and finally said his name was Bob, and he was trying to gather enough money to by a gift for someone he cared a lot about. He went on to say if I would lend him five dollars, he would pay me back ten dollars as soon as he could. Of course I didn't believe him, but I told him I would give him five dollars if he would spend it on something to eat, and not on booze. As I handed him the money, he shook my hand, promising over and over to pay me back. As I turned to walk back to my vehicle, I told him not to worry about paying me back, just not to waste the money on booze.

Time passed and I had pretty much forgotten about my night encounter with Bob. I hadn't seen him in several weeks, and just figured I'd seen the last of him. Then, one night about 2:00 a.m., I was called out for the second time that night. The train dispatcher advised that he had a track indication at north Fort Worth. I arrived at the location, received authority to hy-rail the track and began my track inspection.

I soon found the problem: a piece of pipe lying across both rails. With spotlight and spike maul handle in hand, I walked over to the pipe and picked it up. Tied to the middle of the pipe was an envelope. Inside the envelope there was a ten dollar bill and a note that said, "Sorry it took so long. Thank you, and God Bless."

I was amazed. It just goes to show that things and people aren't always the way they seem. I kept an eye out for ol' Bob for awhile, but I never saw him again. I imagined all kind of good things about Bob. I just hope some of them were true.

SPANN

He was a man with religion, although I never heard him pray. I never heard him tell a joke, but he was funny and would smile at yours. He was a big man with hands of steel, a champion's champion, but not a trophy or plaque displayed. He was the boss's boss but never did he announce the fact, nor did he ever drive a new car. He loved to go fishing and was very good at it, though he would never claim to be a fisherman. He's gone now. Everything prepaid, no funeral, no memorial service, because he wanted it that way. No attorneys needed because everything he had ever purchased was purchased under his sweet wife's name.

In late 1978, I was working as the young safety officer for the southern division of the Santa Fe, headquartered in Temple, Texas. We had just received a new superintendent by the name of Bill Spann. I was in my office gathering facts and figures concerning our safety program and performance, in the event I should be summoned by the superintendent to review the program. I had files and papers scattered everywhere in the office when the phone rang. It was the superintendent's secretary. The superintendent wanted to see me as soon as possible.

In a frenzy, I gathered my files, adjusted my tie, put on my coat and nervously stumbled up the stairs with files tucked under both arms, ready to answer any safety-related question. As I arrived at his office, his secretary told me to go on in. I walked into his office and Mr. Spann was sitting behind his huge desk talking on the phone. I stood nervously for what seemed like forever, when he looked up and motioned for me to sit down.

After a few minutes, he hung up the phone, stood up, walked from behind the desk and shook my hand. As I stood in front of this distinguished, silver headed gentleman, all I could think as he shook my hand was "Wow, what a grip!" His hand was rough, calloused and had the grip of a vise, not a hand that I would envision belonging to the head of an operating division of the Santa Fe railroad.

"So, you're the division safety supervisor. I've heard good things about you," he said. "Briefly go over our safety performance and tell me about what you have in place for a safety/accident prevention program," he continued.

I cleared my throat and began rattling off statistics and standings and the safety programs I had in place to hopefully reduce our injuries and instill a new pride in our safety performance. He sat, leaning back in his chair, and listened to my every word without interruption. As I staggered to a finish, Mr. Spann said that it sounded very ambitious. He added if I ever ran into a problem with support from the field employees or with other supervision, let him know and it would be taken care of.

He then rose from his chair, told his secretary he didn't want to be disturbed for a bit, and closed his office door. I had only been in management for a very short time and had yet to adjust to being a manager myself, so when he closed that door I felt like I would surely suffocate. He slowly walked behind his desk, leaned back in his throne, I mean chair, and said, "I understand you are a fisherman and that you always catch a lot of fish on weekends."

Being that most supervisors came into the office on weekends and met with the superintendent for coffee and discussions, I figured I was about to change my weekend schedule, and it wouldn't include fishing. But I didn't see any point in making excuses, so I told him that I did go fishing on most weekends and I did usually catch fish. I hastily added that I always carried my pager, I was always available for work, and that I didn't drink coffee.

He smiled and then asked, "Just where do you catch all these fish?"

"Lake Belton. Just a twenty minute trip from my house and I can be fishing," I answered.

He began asking me questions. "What kind of fish do you catch?"

"What do you fish with?" "Do you have a boat?"

A little more relaxed than before, I answered all his questions. He told me he loved to fish and even had an old bass boat. Most all his fishing over the past twenty years had been up on the lakes of Minnesota and he wasn't sure how well that would translate to Texas fishing. I told him I would be happy to get him a lake map and mark it for him. He seemed very appreciative as I left his office, a little more relaxed and happy to still have a job.

As I walked back into my office, the road foreman of engines, Bob Gaines, who shared the office, had a grin from ear to ear. "Well, did you ask the boss to go fishing?" he asked.

I told him no, that I had not asked the Superintendent to go fishing.

"The boss asked me about fishing around this area and I told him you were the person to talk to. I can't believe you didn't ask him to go fishing. That's the reason he called you up there," Bob continued.

"Well, I never gave a thought to asking the Superintendent to go fishing. I did tell him I would bring him a map of the lake. I'll ask him then," I answered, thinking to myself I was too far down the totem pole to be rubbing elbows with the top dog.

I rushed out to the local sporting goods store, purchased a map and returned to the office to mark all my prime fishing locations. I then rushed up the stairs not having any idea how you go about asking the superintendent to go fishing. As I reached his office, I noticed the door was closed, so I sat next to his secretary's desk and asked how long it would be before I could see the boss. He said Mr. Spann had appointments for the rest of the afternoon meeting with union dignitaries and other division officials. I told the secretary it wasn't important. I would talk to him another day.

I was actually relieved as I returned to my office. At least I wouldn't have to worry about this fishing invitation for another day or so. I had no more than settled into my office when the door opened and in stepped Mr. Spann. "You looking for me?" he asked.

I stuttered and hem hawed around for a few seconds, but was finally able to spit out that I had the lake map I had mentioned to him. He seemed anxious to see it as I spread it over my desk. I pointed out all the dos and don'ts on the map, and he asked some surprisingly good questions for a person who had spent as much time as he had up north. We finished our map discussions and he sat down in a chair in front of my desk. "Well, Mr. Spann, if you would like to go fishing sometime, I'd be glad to take you," I finally blurted out.

"You want to take my boat or yours?" he asked.

I told him we could take my boat.

"How 'bout Saturday morning? What time will I need to be ready?" he asked.

That's the way it went the day I met Superintendent Bill Spann. Little did I know then how much of an effect he would have on me. It didn't take long for me, as well as others who were fortunate enough to work with him, to see Bill Spann had a wealth of knowledge, he worked hard and he enjoyed life. He was a firm but fair leader who put up no false fronts.

Work, and maintaining a smooth operating railroad, was always a priority with Bill Spann, but it was not his only priority. He believed in enjoying life and if the railroad permitted, we went fishing on weekends. This was a time before cell phones, but he always carried a packset radio with all the railroad frequencies. When we went to the lake, about five miles away, he would always go by the chief dispatcher's office and tell him, "I'll be on my packset," and the chief would know that meant he was heading to the lake.

Along with my office, on the bottom floor of the old Santa Fe depot in Temple, there were a half dozen or so other supervisors' offices. When I was in town, most mornings around ten and afternoons around three, the other officials as well as a few of the clerks from up in the superintendent's office would meet in my office for coffee break. To make things interesting we would all put a dollar in the "pot" and either play guess the number between one and a million or play liars' poker. Whoever won the pot bought the drinks.

Well, one afternoon, we were all gathered in my office with our dollar bills in hand when Mr. Spann walked in. I've never seen dollar bills disappear so fast. He asked what was going on and I told him we were fixin' to see who was going to buy the drinks. Mr. Spann said he was in and asked how we determined who the buyer was. I swallowed real hard and said, "Liars' poker!"

With that, Mr. Spann said, "Pull them dollars back out, boys, and let's get this show on the road."

I'm not sure, but it seems like Mr. Spann won that pot. For about fifteen minutes we were a bunch of railroaders laughing, talking and enjoying each other's company. Instead of the superintendent, several railroad officials and a few clerks, we were just folks enjoying a break from work. From that point on, when in town, Mr. Spann would come downstairs for break. You could hear him coming down the hall, knocking on doors and hollering, "Come on down to Terry's office!"

There were other things that put Mr. Spann in a league of his own. Before his tenure began, previous superintendents would have big managers/officials parties about every three months or so, as well as at Christmas. Mr. Spann stopped those parties, saying that we all saw each other way too much at work as it was, and it didn't make sense to require us to spend our family time together also. He also didn't feel it was right for officials to go out drinking and partying when they were subject to be called to work anytime.

Also, the company paid for the superintendent's membership at the Temple Country Club. Bill Spann cancelled that membership, saying the money could be better spent some other way.

Even simple things set him apart from other high ranking officers. He would always introduce himself as Bill Spann. Not Superintendent Spann or Bill Spann, Superintendent. He once told me that it was not necessary to tell folks what your title is, that most already knew, especially if you're doing your job the way it should be. There were many times when he learned of a person who had an illness in the family, a death or tragedy of some sort and he would tell them not to worry about the railroad or their job, to take whatever time they needed to take care of their family.

Time passed. Weekend fishing trips, when we weren't working, became a regular event. If Mr. Spann was going out on a tour of the division, or if there was a derailment or accident of some kind, he would call me and ask me to travel with him if I was available. Each trip was always a learning experience. He would always explain his thought process and would ask me questions, not because he didn't know the answer but to make sure I did. Of course another benefit of traveling with Mr. Spann was that we never drove past a sporting goods store without going in and checking out the fishing lures.

As the years passed and Mr. Spann came closer to retirement, he would call down to my office occasionally and ask if I was busy. Of course I would always say yes, very busy. Then he would tell me to go home for lunch and instead of coming back, load up my boat and meet him at the lake. I would always say, "You're the boss!"

He loved the lake, and he loved to fish. As we sat out on beautiful Lake Belton that particular afternoon he leaned back and said, "Even though we don't have assigned hours at work, I guess, technically, we are screwing the company. But one thing is for sure, before the end of the week, the company will screw us back."

Later that week, after we had been working a derailment for thirty-six straight hours, Mr. Spann walked by me and simply said, "I told you!"

Many times, as he and I were fishing, the Chief Dispatcher would call on the radio and indicate that there was a need for us back on the railroad. We never hesitated. Even if we were catching, we always loaded the boat and were back at the office in twenty minutes. However, Mr. Spann once said that when he retired, he was going to build a little wooden boat, take it to the lake, place the packset radio on it, push it out into the water, set it on fire and give it a Viking funeral.

Several times before he retired, Mr. Spann asked me if I would be interested in a promotion. Because I was young and had a growing family, I told him I would prefer not to be promoted for now. A promotion would most likely mean relocating, and I would like for the kids to stay in the same school system as long as possible. He said he understood, but to keep it in mind because he felt I was certainly qualified, and he wanted to help me while he was still in a position to do so. I thanked him, and told him that it meant a lot to me for him to have confidence in me.

The day finally came for Mr. Spann to retire. The railroad lost a huge chunk of knowledge, loyalty and integrity that day. In keeping with his history, he refused a retirement party. However, on his last day, he came down to my office for coffee break, and we gave him a huge tackle box loaded with fishing equipment from money his faithful coworkers had given. He cried, right along with most of the rest of us.

For a couple of years after his retirement we still fished on weekends, holidays and vacation days. Then in early 1988 the word came down that the division headquarters in Temple, Texas was going to be shut down, and we were going to be moved to the Dallas/Fort Worth area. It was difficult saying goodbye to the place where I had spent the best ten years of my railroad life. Of course, Mr. Spann was a big reason for that, but there were so many fine, loyal and hard working souls that had given their all to the grand ol' Santa Fe Railroad. Those that did not move with us would be missed.

The years passed more slowly after leaving Temple. I stayed in touch with Mr. Spann, and we still fished when we could get together. I would drive down to Temple and stay with him and his wife Clo on weekends and vacation days. They always made me feel like family. He and I would sit out on the lake. He would ask about the railroad and then just shake his head as I told him of all the changes his beloved railroad was going through.

More time passed, and two heart attacks took their toll on his once strong heart. He was told nearly half of his heart was no longer functioning properly, if at all. It slowed him some with his chores around the house, but only slowed his fishing for awhile. We still met when we could for our occasional fishing outing. He would always tell me which pocket his Nitro pills were in and then never mention his health again.

Yes, he loved to fish. The thing he liked second best was to talk about fishing. If fish were actually caught, that made it even better, no matter who actually caught them. It has been some time ago, although it doesn't seem so, that he went fishing with his mailman, caught a bunch of fish, came home, and put the charger on his boat batteries so they would be charged for the trip the next morning.

He shared supper with his wife, telling her about all the fish they had caught that day. He told her he was going to call Terry, and get him down there while the fish were biting, but went to bed early instead, excited about the next day's fishing trip. He went to sleep happy....and that is the way he left us.

Last night I spent some time with my dear friend. Even though I haven't seen him in many years, I had some much needed conversations with him. It was so nice to see him, enjoy his bright smile and once again hear his slow, low toned words of wisdom.

He hadn't changed since I last saw him, and as he showed me the new fishing lures that he had found in the bargain basket, he spoke. As he spoke I sat and smiled, wishing I had the wisdom and patience of his years.

I woke with a smile and a tear. He was a friend. He shaped a big part of my life, and I miss him terribly. What a wonderful dream!

AW SHUCKS, IT WEREN'T NOTHING

E very railroader has hundreds of tales to tell. If you have a railroader in the crowd, he or she will eventually break out a story or two to entertain. If you have more than one railroader in the bunch you could be there awhile. If the group is made up entirely of railroaders, and you approach the group, you'd better be wearing boots. While most stories have some basis in fact, as they travel from one railroader to another they undergo a little embellishment from time to time.

Every day there is a railroader somewhere on the railroad doing his job, when he is called on to do something that some would think extraordinary. Railroaders, like many other people in other fields of work, are trained in handling and reacting to hundreds of possibilities. I personally know of many individuals on the railroad who have done things that would seem heroic to most of us, but to them were just part of another exciting day on the railroad.

One story involves an old railroader who at one time had climbed the corporate ladder and had ridden his shooting star, but now had begun to climb down that old ladder, trading his shooting star for a slower paced ride of contentment. He had settled into what he thought was a lower profile job as a track supervisor on the BNSF Railway Company. On this particular morning he was sitting near the track in Cleburne, Texas waiting for one more train to pass so he could get on the track and hy-rail to Fort Worth, making his daily inspections. He saw the signal for southbound trains go green, which meant that the train he was waiting on, a loaded coal train with about 120 cars weighing about 16,000 tons, was getting close.

As the old track supervisor sat waiting, he observed a gasoline tanker truck hauling 9000 gallons of fuel leaving a fuel depot about fifty yards from the tracks. As the driver started across the tracks, his trailer dollies, which he had apparently forgotten to raise, struck the crossing, causing the trailer to come unhooked and fall down on the main track. Knowing that the train was near, the track supervisor immediately hit the emergency button on his radio and shouted, "Emergency, emergency, emergency! All trains in the Cleburne area stop movement immediately. There is a fuel tanker stuck on the tracks at the crossing at mile post 317.5." The train dispatcher came on the radio and called for the coal train. The train responded and said that they had heard the broadcast and had placed their train into emergency braking to insure that they would be able to stop short of the truck. The train eventually stopped well short of the truck.

Meanwhile the track supervisor pulled up next to the truck with his emergency strobe lights flashing and tried to calm the truck driver, who was in the process of ramming the trailer over and over trying to recouple with it. The driver finally twisted the drive shaft in two, and now the truck and trailer were both blocking the track. The track supervisor finally was able to calm the driver by assuring him that all trains were stopped and aware of the circumstances. Other than needing to change his britches, the truck driver and all others concerned were okay. After an hour or so, and with the assistance of a couple of heavy-duty wrecker trucks, all was restored to normal operations.

Other than clearing the track of a dozen head of cattle at Crowley, Texas and running a couple of kids off a bridge in Fort Worth, the old track supervisor was able to complete his day as he was expected to do. That evening the old railroader came home, kicked off his boots and headed for his recliner. He gave his wife a big hug and she asked him how his day went. "Pretty much the same old stuff. How was your day?" he said as he sank into the soft confines of contentment.

Day to Day, Year to Year, Boy to Man

PART VI

———————⬥———————

His days back on the ground, so to speak, were not as much a relief as he had anticipated. Many of his bosses were those that had worked for or been trained by him. Many in the field were leery of him because he had been in management. What they didn't realize was that he had ridden his shooting star and wasn't out to impress anybody. He was there to finish his twelve or so years of service to the best of his ability, retire and go home. He worked about eleven more years on a track supervisor job that was on call twenty-four hours a day, seven days a week just as he had been for most of his career. Very seldom did he get to spend an entire night with his wife.

Then the years, along with other physical demands, began to take a toll on his not so old, but not young, body. He became a big contributor to the betterment of several medical organizations. Over a period of years he underwent hernia surgery, eight major knee surgeries, elbow surgery, lower back surgery, had a major heart attack, found out he only had one kidney, and developed type two diabetes. With about a year and a half left to work before full retirement, he was sent for a full medical evaluation. All the previous procedures and ailments were studied. After it also became apparent that his right shoulder joint was in need of complete replacement, it was determined that he should be placed on full disability and granted early retirement from the railroad, which by then had become the Burlington Northern Santa Fe Railroad.

In the beginning there was resentment. After all, all he wanted was to finish the career he had started almost forty years before. However, it didn't take long for him to realize he was born to be retired. It was so nice to lie down with his wife and know that they would wake up together the next morning. It was nice to be at home and awake to watch the ten o'clock news. It was nice to only be on call twenty-four hours a day, seven days a week for his family. It was nice to be able to simply walk into the next room and see his wife anytime he wanted too.

There had been regrets, some of which could be corrected and some not. One of the greatest gifts of retirement is time. Time for the family and time for friends. He soon found that there was a trade-off for having earned this time. The kids, now wives and mothers with families of their own, didn't always have time. He may very well have been the dad that Harry Chapin had in mind when he wrote "Cats In The Cradle." But, he is available now and makes the most of time shared with friends and family.

He is home now. There have been things lost, lessons learned and faith found. He hasn't smiled this much since high school. He has learned that his life involves a lot more than just him. He often goes back to the memories of those who have touched his life and prays that they know how thankful he is. He walks a little slower, he can't throw a ball as far as he once did, and he may forget your name, but his heart beats with the strength gained from those he loves and those who chose to love him.

Yes, he is back home. The days go by much faster now, but the nights allow time for thought and for dreams. He lies in bed, rolls over, gives his sweet wife a kiss and holds her for awhile. Then, sometimes, he closes his eyes and imagines he's lying there listening to the sound of the rustling leaves of the old cottonwood tree outside his open window.

THE END

Did you enjoy Terry's stories? Would you like more?

Be watching for his next book in the A Gathering of Words series:

I'VE BEEN THINKING

Available Summer 2014

Want more Terry?

Keep up with him online at:

Facebook.com/TerryBeckWords

TerryBeckBlog.blogspot.com

Terry is also available for speaking engagements.
Please contact him at terry-beck@att.net.

Turn the page for a sneak peek at
A GATHERING OF WORDS — I'VE BEEN THINKING

A GATHERING OF WORDS

I'VE BEEN THINKING

by TERRY BECK

To Be Released Summer 2014

I'VE BEEN THINKING

I've been thinking, more or less, for a long time. First there was "suggestive inducement thinking." This is where Mom and Pop would point at an object and repeat its name or title over and over and over, until I would finally repeat the word in order to get them to move on to something else. Hopefully, that something else was lunch.

Then, along came "mandatory thinking". This was encountered in the school years where you were required to train in the ability to think, and as a result, actually learn. Then, you where tested and graded on your ability to think, with the results displayed every six weeks for all to see.

Next up was artificially, or "chemically induced" thinking. I really don't think the learning process was involved in this particular era. It seems that this time frame, although rather vague, was filled with, what I felt at the time, extremely imaginative thoughts that were rarely ever transformed into any actual action. I can recall thinking at the time, "Wow, this is really far out. It just doesn't get any cooler than this." Fortunately for me, I managed to pass through this thinking phase relatively undamaged. Now that I think back, I probably didn't really have as much fun as I thought I did.

Finally, I arrived at the "thinking for profit" stage, or labor related thinking. I entered the work force, where I was required to think for pay. I quickly learned that the more I thought and the better my thoughts, the more money my employer was willing to pay me. This phase of the thinking process worked out pretty well for me nearly forty years. Then I got tired of thinking for money. It was becoming obvious that my particular thinking process was becoming obsolete and that my thinking did not involve those I loved as much as it should have. I decided that I was no longer going to think for pay. I retired.

I didn't quit thinking; I just ceased to think for the above mentioned reasons. Now I think just for the heck of it, and I catch myself thinking all the time. I have so much to think about. Some of it is real, some of it is wishful, but all of it is worthwhile. I take journeys back into the past, the joys and the heart breaks, the mistakes and the successes, the family and the friends. I find that my mind and my thinking process are a valuable part of what I am now. I am no longer graded on my thinking abilities. I no longer let chemicals or other artificial products tilt my thinking toward the unreal or unreachable. I no longer think for pay. I think because it is a beautiful place to be. Whether it is experience based, imagination based or a search for a better way, thinking is so easy now.

I realize that there will be challenges both physically and mentally, now and in the future, but currently the world of thought is bright and has endless possibilities. There are so many who have provided the fuel for my dream-filled thought processes. For all who have contributed, I say "Thank you, and I'll be thinking about you"!